How to Live
Nobly and Well

Edward F. Garesché, S.J.

How to Live Nobly and Well

Timeless Principles for Achieving True Success and Lasting Happiness

SOPHIA INSTITUTE PRESS®
Manchester, New Hampshire

How to Live Nobly and Well: Timeless Principles for Achieving True Success and Lasting Happiness is an abridged edition of *The Will to Succeed* (New York: P. J. Kenedy and Sons, 1931) and contains minor editorial revisions to the original text.

Printed in the United States of America

Jacket design by Lorraine Bilodeau

The cover artwork is a detail of Lorenzo Lotto's *Portrait of a Man*, Accademia, Venice, Italy (used with permission of Scala/Art Resource, New York).

Sophia Institute Press®
Box 5284, Manchester, NH 03108
1-800-888-9344
www.sophiainstitute.com

Imprimi potest: Matthew Germing, S.J., *Praepos. Prov.*, Missouri
Nihil obstat: Arthur J. Scanlan, S.T.D., *Censor Librorum*
Imprimatur: Patrick Cardinal Hayes, Archbishop of New York
September 4, 1931

Library of Congress Cataloging-in-Publication Data

Garesché, Edward F. (Edward Francis), 1876-1960.
[Will to succeed]
How to live nobly and well : timeless principles for achieving true success and lasting happiness / Edward F. Garesché.
p. cm.
Originally published: The will to succeed. New York : P. J. Kenedy, 1931.
ISBN 0-918477-16-6 (pbk. : alk. paper)
1. Success. I. Title.
BJ1611.G37 1999
170'.44 — dc21 99-23597 CIP

99 00 01 02 03 04 05 9 8 7 6 5 4 3 2 1

Contents

1

Recognize daily opportunities for success . . . 3

2

Strive for lasting success . . . 7

3

Choose what will improve your character . . . 11

4

Persevere in noble pursuits . . . 17

5

Develop your mind through study . . . 21

6

Learn from your mistakes and failures . . . 25

7

See and imitate the good in others . . . 29

8

Develop good habits . . . 35

9

Let prudence guide your decisions . . . 39

10

Practice justice in all its forms . . . 45

11

Be temperate . . . 49

12

Develop fortitude . . . 53

13

Choose happiness over pleasure . . . 59

14

Learn to do without nonessentials . . . 65

15

Be pleasant in your demeanor and in your actions . . . 69

16

Develop your power of observation . . . 75

17
Be yourself . . . 81

18
Discipline your imagination . . . 85

19
Strengthen your will . . . 91

20
Let reason guide you . . . 95

21
Choose worthwhile amusements . . . 99

22
Take care of your body . . . 103

23
Maintain a healthy mind . . . 107

24
Think kindly of others . . . 111

25
Resist temptations . . . 115

26
Gain mastery over yourself . . . 121

27
Distinguish between true good and false good . . . 125

28
Do not fear what others think . . . 129

29
Use criticism prudently . . . 133

30
Rely on your will, not on your feelings . . . 139

31
Have confidence in yourself . . . 143

32
Build a noble character . . . 147

Edward F. Garesché, S.J. . . . 151

How to Live
Nobly and Well

Chapter One

Recognize daily opportunities for success

As you stand on the threshold of the future, what is before you? You are an unknown quantity even to yourself. Your coming days are like a blank check in which you must fill the significant figures. They are like an empty page on which you must write the record of nobleness or ignominy or mere dull mediocrity. You have within you the stuff of heroes, and you have also within you instincts and tendencies that, yielded to, will make you a degraded criminal. You feel the pull of opposite tendencies: now you dream of great things; now you are tugged downward by impulses of which you are ashamed.

But you are the captain of your own soul; you are the arbiter of your own destiny. God and man both give you a fair chance, a noble opportunity. God has endowed you with a free will, the divine prerogative of choosing between good and evil. He has given you a body and a soul, both excellent and beneficial, the climax of His visible creation. He has brought you into being, without a past, but with a splendid future, if you will seize it by your free and virtuous effort.

At the same time, you cannot be really free without having the choice between good and evil, and if you deliberately choose what is evil and base, you may have it and, with it, the dark consequence of a ruined life, lost opportunities, and dismal failure. You have everything that you need from God to become a noble person, upright, God-fearing, respected, and successful, in the right meaning of success.

In what land on earth do you have brighter opportunities, greater rewards of service, a finer field of manly effort, than in our country today? You are the heir of all the centuries in literature, in art, in science, in commerce, and in every avenue of achievement. True, the world is full of temptations and opportunities for evil, as it always was, but it is full of far greater opportunities, far more multiplied chances, for good. If you choose to invest your life as you should, you have a field of sublime excellence for that investment.

Your feet are set at the entrance to a great battlefield where the victors are all heroes. With courage, confidence, hopefulness, and steadfastness, you are sure to win, because you have nothing to fear but your own weakness, your own cowardice.

It is with a great desire to help you, to cheer you, and to influence you for good that these pages are written. They are intended to give you the advantage of the experience of the past and the observation of many people concerning the true principles of success in life. And as all people are, in a way, continually beginning, making a new start each morning and each new year, these thoughts will be useful for anyone, we trust, who takes up this book. "While there is life, there is hope," as an old writer has said. "Men are made of clay, and clay, though it is easily broken, is likewise easily mended."

Even those who have lost the opportunities of youth and have hitherto made failures of their lives, may, at any moment, begin to struggle upward. They may recapture, by courage and resolve, the first glow of youthful virtue, and we trust that the thoughts contained in these pages will give them courage, light, and strength.

Success in life rests on definite principles and depends on each man's free choice. According to those principles, it can be surely gained or surely lost, according to the workings of the great laws of human nature. Choose rightly, and you will make a success of life.

Chapter Two

Strive for lasting success

Before we speak of the means to achieve success, we should form a clear idea for ourselves as to what success means, in what it consists, for we cannot discuss the way sensibly unless we know where we are going. Everyone who is not a fool desires success in life, but many fail to achieve it, even with their utmost effort, because they have not rightly conceived what really constitutes success.

A successful life is a life that achieves its purpose. Such a life is a happy one, even though its way may pass through suffering and difficulty, because happiness is one thing and pleasure another, and a person may have great pleasure and still be very unhappy, just as he may lack pleasure almost entirely and still be very happy.

What is the purpose of life? The chorus of all generations of mankind, the general conclusion of history, is that the purpose of life is to do one's duty to God and man, to make the most of one's opportunities of service, to live virtuously, and thus enjoy the happiness here and hereafter that comes from such performance of duty. I say this is the final conclusion of mankind. It is true that there are many individuals who put success in various forms of achievement.

Some people look on success as the acquirement of great sums of money, and the reason they judge thus is that money means power; it means the acquirement of property and influence and the enjoyment of good things of this world. Hence, when men put success in business achievement, they confess that the good things of this world seem to them the way to happiness.

But is this so? A little reflection will show that it is not.

Money is a means to an end, and very often a necessary means, because a man must live decently and must support his family, if he has one. But some of the greatest failures in history have been those who have accumulated huge sums of money, but who have lacked moral principle and have been false to their duty; wherefore, they made gigantic failures. The greatest persons of history have often been poor in material things, but they have always been rich in principle, in devotion to duty; otherwise they would have been not truly great.

There are others who have put success in the acquirement of honor or reputation, and here again they were wrong, because honor in itself is not so much in the person himself as in the thoughts of others. Honor does not bring a person lasting happiness. Many a one has achieved immense reputation and then left, in his own writings, the record of his disillusionment and disappointment. It is not those who have achieved renown who are truly fortunate and happy, but those who have deserved honor by their virtue.

What has been said of honor may be said, too, of power and influence. These are not the real rewards of life. Here, again, many a man has succeeded in rising to great heights and yet made a failure of his life. Remember the great Napoleon at St.

Helena. He had climbed and fought to the peak of human greatness, and he left behind a name that will endure for many generations. Yet his career recalls at its end the saying of Solomon: "Vanity of vanities, and all is vanity."[1]

Rather, it is the leading of a virtuous and upright life, the performance of one's duties to God and man, the making the most of every opportunity for service, and the harmonious development of every faculty that make for real success in life and that lead to happiness here and a greater happiness hereafter. You have only a few years in which to realize in your own person this end of dutiful service. To realize it, you may have to "scorn delights, and live laborious days";[2] you may be obliged to forget friendships, amusements, and even success, when these are against your conscience and your duty. But in this way, and in this way alone, lie true success and happiness.

[1] Eccles. 1:2. The biblical quotations in these pages are based on the Douay-Rheims edition of the Old and New Testaments. — Ed.

[2] John Milton, "Lycidas," line 64.

Chapter Three

Choose what will improve your character

By what a man is, he influences others, sways them, helps them, and impresses them. Knowledge is a great possession and a necessary one for success in life, but character and principle are far more needful. Many men of great knowledge have gone down into contempt or oblivion because of their wretched character, their mean personality, whereas very simple folk, with little education, have become heroes, leaders of men, because of their noble character and personality. You yourself are immensely impressed and moved by the personality, the character, of those with whom you come in contact. In like manner, all your life long, your own character will have its inevitable effect upon others, for better or worse, according as your character is noble, kindly, and steadfast, or the opposite.

Your character is made up of various elements. First of all, there are the natural tendencies in you, the inherited characteristics you possess. Then there are the habits you have acquired by your own repeated actions, which form a second nature and can change, round out, or tone down your inherited characteristics. Finally, there is the environment in which you find yourself, or put yourself, and this also has a powerful effect on your personality. The sum of these three things results in what we call your character.

Thus, for example, you may have been born with a lively, active disposition, or you may have been born with a tendency to be slow and quiet. But, over and above your natural disposition, you have a whole series of habits, which you acquired by the repetition of actions. Every time you got angry, the habit of anger increased, but every time you subdued and controlled your anger, the habit of self-control grew greater within you. Every time you yielded to selfishness, you became just a little more selfish, but each time you performed an act of generosity, you grew a little more generous. Thus, to your dying day, action increases the habit or tendency from which it springs, much as a muscle grows stronger and stronger by use and weaker and weaker by disuse. Now, you can change, improve, or degrade your character to a marvelous degree by voluntary and repeated actions, either of good or of evil. So every deed you do brings its own reward or punishment, in that it strengthens the proneness to good in you, if it is good, or increases the tendency to evil in you, if it is evil.

One who constantly and systematically does what is right can change a vicious, warped, disagreeable natural character into one of great kindness and virtue; whereas one who is born with a very good and genial disposition can spoil it by yielding to unkindness and other forms of evil. It is immensely important for you to grasp this principle and act on it. If there is anything in you that you judge to be bad, dangerous, or an impediment to true success, begin now and, day after day, act against that bad tendency. Little by little, it will grow weaker the more you oppose it, and the contrary habit of goodness will increase. After long effort, you will become as strong as you were once weak and as dependable and constant as you were once changeable and unreliable.

True, it requires a very strong will to go against our natural inclinations. But no one is perfect by nature. Noble and great characters are all made so by the constant repetition of virtuous actions. "To thine own self be true, and it will follow, as the night the day, thou canst not then be false to any man!"[3]

The third element influencing our character and personality is environment. The people we associate with, the work we do, the amusements we seek, and the books we read all have a continual and powerful influence on our character. When you form friendships, when you read books, when you engage in amusements, it may seem to you that it makes very little difference how you choose, provided you suit yourself. But every one of these things has a tremendous and lasting influence on your personality. If you seek people who are refined, upright, high principled, noble, and humane, you yourself tend to become like them. If you choose friends who are rough, coarse, vicious, and unprincipled, you will assimilate yourself to them.

So, too, the amusements you select tend to mold your mind and feelings to their likeness. Any entertainment that is degraded, coarse, or cheap cheapens or coarsens your imagination and your disposition. Any amusement that is elevated and noble elevates and ennobles you. This is eminently true of books, in which you associate with people of other times and encounter other people's thoughts. If you take up a trashy, especially a vile, book and allow its trashy and vile thoughts to pass

[3] William Shakespeare, *Hamlet,* Act 1, scene 3.

through your mind, their imprint will be left permanently on your character. The memory really never forgets anything; the imagination never loses anything that is thrown into its vast receptacle.

You will have to exercise real self-discipline, sometimes hard self-denial, to curb the lower part of your nature and follow your higher impulses in choosing friends, amusements, and books. But the sacrifice and the effort are as worthwhile as a noble life is worthwhile.

Now, everyone has it within his own power to choose his friends, to choose his recreations, and to choose his reading, just as he has it within his own power to resist evil habits and thus to diminish them in his character, and to follow good lines of action and thus to cultivate virtues. There is no other way to have a fine character, a worthwhile personality, except by this continual effort, self-discipline, and self-sacrifice.

Read the autobiography of Benjamin Franklin, and you will learn how steadfastly he set about cultivating his character. He studied his own disposition and noted what good qualities and what bad tendencies he possessed. He drew up a regular plan for rooting out faults and cultivating virtues. At the beginning of the week, he would set himself to the task of lessening the number of faults of, let us say, undue self-assertiveness, and whenever he found himself to have been proud, opinionated, or disputatious, he would mark down the fault in a book, so as to notice how the record increased or decreased from the beginning to the end of the week.

In this way, he grappled with, and overcame one by one, the outstanding defects of his disposition. At the same time, he deliberately associated with those who were considered wise and virtuous, and he read books that gave him solid information and help. Thus, his singular success in life and the immense influence he exercised on his own and succeeding generations were the results of tireless industry in the formation of his character, by cultivating good habits and securing for himself a favorable environment. His achievements were a notable proof of how a man can mold and better his own character.

Those who really succeed in life can find no other way but the way of self-discipline and self-control, which is also the way to the greatest happiness possible on earth.

Chapter Four

Persevere in noble pursuits

Someone has defined *courage* as a dogged determination to go on. More than most young people realize, this is essential for success. To keep on trying, hammering at difficulties, pressing forward, over rough ground and smooth, seeking an objective through thick and thin, is the way to succeed. The race is not to the swift, nor the battle to the strong,[4] but rather to the man who will keep on trying. Everlasting perseverance, the quality of getting up after every fall and coming back after every blow, wins at last. Discouragement is the most fatal obstacle to success. Those who never know they are beaten, never are beaten. Defeat has no power to detain them. After each calamity, they come back, stronger than before. But the one who believes he is beaten, has actually lost the battle, even if he still has enough resources and enough strength to win a victory.

The army that can persevere, fighting through in spite of reverses, wins the day. This is an immensely important conviction for young people to bring home to themselves at the beginning of their career. Find out what you want, select a

[4] Cf. Eccles. 9:11.

worthy objective, and keep on struggling toward it, and you will inevitably succeed, provided you have life and strength and are aiming at some achievement you are capable of accomplishing. Keep at it, spend continuous effort, and you will achieve what you wish.

Prudence must, of course, direct even your perseverance. A man who keeps on under a strain, and insists on getting results quickly, may wear himself out before he reaches his goal. There is a sort of perseverance that consists in always coming back to your objective, seeking it again and again, in spite of weariness, in spite of enforced rest, in spite even of the sickness of hope deferred. This intermittent perseverance, as we may call it, this quality of returning to effort in the same direction, is often more prudent than a headlong and continuous drive that wears out your energy. It is not so much getting results quickly that counts as keeping at a reasonable degree of effort in the same direction. This is what we mean by perseverance.

The word *perseverance* comes from the Latin *per*, which means "through," and *severus*, which means "strict." There is a good deal of wisdom in this derivation. A persevering person is one who is strict with himself, who is hard on himself, who disregards his natural feelings and weariness, his cravings and grudges, and hammers through in spite of his own weakness. The greatest obstacles to perseverance are often not the difficulties you meet from without, but the difficulties that come from within.

If you are strong enough to overcome yourself, to disregard your own weariness and discouragement, and to subdue your own indecision and push straight to the forward line in spite of your own weaknesses, then you are going to persevere. It is not what other people do to you, or what events do to you, that keeps you from persevering, but what you experience inwardly of weakness and changeableness.

Perseverance is chiefly rooted in an unwavering will. It is a determination to keep up the fight, to go on with the struggle, to pay the price fully and courageously.

Of course, one must be sure that what he is making a persevering effort to achieve is really worth having. "Be sure you are right, then go ahead!" advises the homely saying. Anyone who starts out after something that is really not worth having is wasting the fine quality of perseverance. He is like one who pays a great price for a gold coin that is gold only on the surface, or like those luckless explorers of old times who came to this country and gathered huge quantities of copper pyrites, "fool's gold," as it is called, and took it home under the impression that their hard-gotten cargo was made up of precious metal.

Every ambition and every aspiration, especially in youth, ought to be assayed and tested with the touchstone of genuine worth. Many a young person makes a failure of his life because he sets out after something that he conceives to be very valuable and spends his life trying to get it, only to regret it later.

Some make wealth their objective and sacrifice everything else to get it. The gain, they find, is not worth the battle. Money does not bring them the satisfaction they thought it would, and they have lost things much more precious in trying to get rich. When money is made only a means to an end, as it should be, it may be good to persevere in trying to get it. But money for its own sake is not worth trying for; it is sure to disappoint you.

As we observed before, the same thing can be said of fame or reputation. Too many young persons with fine talents and native gifts conceive an immense ambition to be famous. Their great objective is glory, and they will do anything to achieve it, but after a time, they find that glory is vain and deceptive. They are not satisfied when they have achieved it, and all their efforts to that end appear to them as wasted or worse than wasted.

One could make very similar reflections concerning pleasure, but with still more emphasis. One who makes pleasure his objective is likely to become the most wretched of mortals, because pleasure is not an end in itself, but only a means of helping us to further ends. It is a passing reward given to recreate and cheer us, but, pursued for its own sake, it becomes a source of satiety and disgust. As Socrates wisely said of those who pursue sensual pleasures especially, "They itch to scratch, and they scratch to itch" — a pitifully vicious circle.

The wise person will make the gaining of honor, wealth, and pleasure secondary to the living of a virtuous life of upright kindness and service. In this way, he will achieve real happiness so far as it is possible for anyone to attain it here, and hereafter he will arrive at that full contentment and satisfaction which is the reward of perseverance in right living, justice, and kindness.

Chapter Five

Develop your mind through study

The intent concentration of the mind on a problem, which focuses upon it all our capacities for intelligence and seeks to comprehend it and weigh it in all its aspects and relations, is what we mean by *study*. The word comes from the Latin *studium*, meaning "eagerness," because eagerness of the will for truth, for fact, for honest decision, must lie at the root of all our study.

There is a good deal of superficial thinking nowadays. People are lazy in intellect. They wish to get along with as little study as possible. They jump to conclusions and seek information by shortcuts. The intent concentration required to solve problems is too much for their lazy minds. Yet, the one who really wishes to succeed must train his will, his memory, and his imagination so that he can truly study, can truly concentrate his intellect on a problem so as to solve it as it should be solved.

If you examine critically the careers of great men, you will find that, almost without exception, they depend for their success to a very great degree on their power of concentration, of attention and decision — in other words, on their power of study. The ideal person is one who is equally balanced in heart, intelligence, and will, so that he is able at the same time to will strongly, to feel tenderly, and to decide vigorously and carefully. One who slips or slurs over any one of these elements of greatness really destroys his chances of becoming a person of fine achievement. The intelligence is necessary as a guide to action, the will is necessary as the rudder to steer the ship, and the feelings are needful in order that a person may not be a mere automaton, a mechanical and self-centered being, but may be deeply human, and rightly humane in the true sense of that noble word.

Now, perhaps strong will and good feelings are more common than effective study, the concentration of the mind and the functioning of the intelligence that goes into the heart of the subject to discover the objective truth. This much is certain: many more persons seem to have good hearts than have good heads, and the errors and misfortunes of mankind come much more from ignorance and stupidity than from malice. Those who deliberately and constantly apply their intelligence in an unbiased way to the solution of their problems are much more likely to live a happy life and achieve real success than those who slur over the need for study and try to make a strong will or dogged determination take the place of earnest thought and intelligent decision.

The intellect is a faculty that may be strengthened, made accurate and dependable, just as may any other of our faculties. Exercising the intellect thus makes it alert, dependable, correct, and enduring. If you observe successful persons, you will find that they give time to quiet reflection, or, perhaps, that they have developed the faculty of thinking deeply and accurately as they go. They discuss, weigh opinions, and look at both sides of a question — in other words, they exercise their intellect as a guide in their decisions.

Unthinking people sometimes complain that those who draw the largest salaries in great corporations seem to do the least work. The man who works with his hands has to observe regular hours and be on duty at a certain time. Those who have less important positions in the offices are likewise required to work longer hours. But the chief of the whole corporation, the man who makes the important decisions, who really guides and directs the whole enterprise, is very often on duty for fewer hours than any of his employees.

Such a man may come in late in the morning and spend only a few hours at his desk, but he is the thinking part of the corporation; the rest are working with their hands or minds in merely subordinate capacities. He is the one who has to take the responsibility for grave decisions, to frame new policies or enforce old ones. In other words, he is the brains of the enterprise, and he receives his salary, not for doing tasks, but for thinking and deciding.

Thus, it is the man who can think and decide who has the faculty of concentration and of study, who succeeds, and he who lacks this faculty is apt to fail. Since, therefore, you aspire after success, learn to study. Examine every one of your problems with fair and frank intelligence. Try to put away mere conjectures and to avoid the habit of jumping at decisions without taking the trouble to reason about them. Insist on cultivating the power of serious thought. You will thus be giving yourself a great advantage over the light-minded and the lazy-minded, for you will not be led by mere feelings or by half-truths, but by the clear light of a strong and sure intellect.

Chapter Six

Learn from your mistakes and failures

The one who knows how to profit by his own errors is the one who makes a success of life. To be discouraged over your mistakes is foolish. To disregard them is equally unwise. To face them fearlessly and try to learn from them how to avoid a mistake next time is the part of wisdom. When one begins any important task, he ought to watch carefully so as to avoid the errors that he has made in the past. He ought to learn from every new error how to diminish his mistakes in the future.

There are many classes of persons on life's highway with whom you must rub elbows as you go. Some of them are dullards who care for nothing, notice nothing, and keep on making one mistake after another. You should not imitate them or fall into their company. Others are dogged, self-sufficient persons who insist they are right, even when they are wrong, wishing not even to admit their errors, much less to profit by them. These people also, and their methods, you ought to avoid. There are also the discouraged people who plod along, beaten and weary. They have admitted to themselves that life is a failure, that their mistakes have overwhelmed them. Far from learning from their errors, they have lain down under the burden of their own weakness. You should avoid also following the example of these people, who fail in life for want of courage and wisdom.

Then there are the wise, brave folk, who never let a mistake pass unnoticed or uncorrected, but who use each error as a means of avoiding similar errors in the future. These men and women learn more from their mistakes than from their successes. They keep a constant watch on themselves without discouragement, without foolish fear, trying always to see themselves and their work as they are, admitting their own shortcomings and guarding against them, satisfied with partly succeeding in avoiding the mistakes of today by remembering the mistakes of yesterday, and using the mistakes of today to make the work of tomorrow a little more excellent, in the sight of God and man.

These latter people are the ones who really make the most of life's opportunities, who are worthy citizens, who are good friends, who keep their spirits sweet and unspoiled even in the midst of life's inevitable disappointments. Errors do not discourage them, do not make them desperate, and do not leave them as ignorant and as careless as before. But they learn constantly in the hard but efficacious school of experience, and day after day, year after year, they grow wiser, better, and more dependable, by means of observing and correcting the faults and errors of the past.

It requires plenty of real courage and honesty to be sincere with oneself. There are many men and women who, their whole lives long, are afraid to stand face-to-face with their own mistakes and with the defects of their own character. They deceive themselves about themselves. They actually contrive, in spite of daily experience, to remain blind to their faults and shortcomings. A most dangerous deception is self-deception. It is only by seeing ourselves as we are that we can remake and perfect our own character. Those who are afraid to acknowledge their errors, who shirk from confessing even to themselves that they have been wrong and that they have defects, will hardly grow any better. Young people in particular ought to try to acquire, from their first beginnings in the rude ways of life, the habit of sincerity and frankness in judging their own character and their own deeds.

You can learn a great deal from others about your own character, especially about its weak places and the errors that you commit, and this is very valuable information. When you make others angry by your faults, they are likely, in the moment of anger, to give you splendid criticism, which is the frank expression of their shrewd observation about you. In their calmer moments, many people will never trouble to admonish you. In fact, they would shrink from telling you just what they think about you, because they fear to give you pain. But when one of your defects has angered them, the moment of irritation overcomes their reticence, and they blurt out just what they think of you, frankly and without disguise.

Now, just as you can judge of others much more shrewdly and correctly than you can judge of yourself, so others can judge of you better than they can recognize their own defects and shortcomings. What they say about you frankly, in moments of irritation, may not be quite true, but it is usually very illuminating. Never grow discouraged at such unfavorable comments. You may often say to yourself that they are excessive and motivated by anger. Therefore, you may not be so bad as your angry friend may indicate. But there is usually a grain of truth even in the midst of their vexed exaggeration. As a blow with steel strikes fire out of flint, so the sharp touch of anger sometimes strikes truth out of a heart.

At all events, these criticisms that others pass on you are worth considering and studying. If, after thinking over the sharp words said to you, you honestly judge that there was no truth in them at all, you may well disregard them. But if you find that, even though they were intemperate, still there was some basis of fact in the criticism, profit by it. Any light shed on your character and its defects, from whatever source it comes, ought to be welcome, provided it is true and honest light. A good thing to remember for real success in life is not to keep your self-love unwounded and preserve an excessive good opinion of yourself, but rather to see yourself as you really are, so that you may profit by your errors to improve your character.

If you acknowledge your mistakes and learn by them, by that very fact the errors will be atoned for and will no longer be a subject of regret and shame. The defects in your character that are admitted and corrected will be a source of credit to you. But the errors that you deny and gloss over and fail to profit by, or atone for, will someday, sooner or later, rise up to vex and shame you. To err is human and everyone makes some mistakes, but by learning from our mistakes, we cooperate with God in building up a noble character.

Chapter Seven

See and imitate the good in others

Whether you like it or not, you are sure to imitate other people. The impulse to follow the example of others is so strong in us that we obey it unconsciously. We begin as little children, copying those around us, and we imitate the bad in them as well as the good.

But now that you are older, you can choose what to imitate. On that choice depends, to a great degree, your character and your destiny. If you observe and imitate the good and choose to copy the good qualities of those with whom you associate, you will be, in the old comparison, like the bee that gathers honey from every flower and leaves the poison. On the other hand, if you do not choose carefully whom to imitate, you will collect bad qualities and accentuate the faults of your character.

To have a clear, alert, and fair mind, and to judge men's good qualities rightly are of supreme importance, especially to the young. Do not be deceived by appearances; do not adopt wrong standards of conduct. Some people have showy, specious, false characters that make a good impression at first, but there is no substance to their personality. Others do not attract or impress us much at first, but they improve on acquaintance. They wear well; they have solid characters, fine hearts, good minds, and consistent principles. Those are the ones to imitate. Many a young person has gone wrong and wrecked his whole life because he did not see truly and judge rightly whom to follow, but let himself be carried away by his first impressions, his feelings, or his emotions.

All human beings have some good qualities, of course, and by observing their good qualities and imitating them, and recognizing their mistakes and avoiding them, you can steer your way safely through the difficult seas of human character.

It is told of one young man who made a supreme success in life, that he deliberately noted the good qualities of all those around him. He would jot down such notes as this: "I like A's pleasant, kindly smile; I am going to try to imitate it. I like B's everlasting willingness to oblige and serve other people, and I am going to try to make it my own. I like C's custom of punctuality and reliableness, and I am going to try to be the same myself. D's fine mental culture appeals to me, and I want to be like him in that respect." In this way, the young man deliberately emulated, and made his own by constant practice, the very best that he saw around him.

No human character is quite ideal, but every one has some divine spark of goodness in it. By taking all the good characteristics of those around you, you can build up the ideal of a perfect character, just as, by taking all the unpleasant characteristics of each one, you could create a sort of monster.

One advantage of this method of looking for the good qualities of others and imitating them is that it brings out by contrast your own imperfections. If you study the best in others and compare that best with your own corresponding traits, you will feel humble and be stirred up to be better. There is hardly anyone around you who does not surpass you in something. Yet, you have the divine gift of free will, by which you can continually practice and aspire after the good qualities that others possess, without envying them and without taking anything away from those whom you imitate. This is the very opposite of jealousy, that wicked and hideous monster of vice, which observes the good in other people and is saddened by it. Your keen observation must pick out the good qualities in others not in order to envy them, but to rejoice in them and imitate them. Thus, you will multiply their goodness and gain by it, by becoming like them in that particular characteristic in which they most excel.

Suppose you had the power of taking for yourself the best qualities you see in others. With what keen interest you would study each one's character in order to choose the very best trait you would find there. You would weigh each one's personal charm and try to find out on what it depended. Here you would see that it was the result of a spirit of great kindness and interest in others, and you would choose that characteristic. There you would see that it came chiefly from a finely cultured mind, and you would make that quality your own. Another man's influence over others and power to do good to them has come, you would perceive, from his deep conscientiousness and faithfulness to duty, and you would make those qualities your own.

Now, in literal truth, you can obtain to a degree any one of these things, by wanting it earnestly enough and seeking it persistently enough. The measure of your right judgment in seeing clearly the best that is in others and your strong will in disciplining yourself to acquire their particular excellences will be the measure of your success in getting the best that they possess.

When thus trying to acquire the best characteristics of mankind, you need not confine yourself to the people you actually know. Through the magnificent works of literature, you can associate with marvelous familiarity with the great minds, the noble hearts, and the shining characters of all history. Saints and heroes of hundreds of years offer you their knowledge and companionship on the shelves of libraries.

This is one of the greatest blessings of a love of reading: it brings us into communion with the choicest spirits of all the ages. Entering a library in a thoughtful and reverent mood, we can stretch forth our hands and bid this, that, and the other of the most excellent of mankind to speak to us. In great books, we find a revelation of human character in its excellence and nobility that our personal experiences could never offer us. The ordinary dealings of everyday life are sometimes like a game of hide-and-seek, in which men and women carefully conceal even their own excellences. They are reluctant to show the finest depths of their characters. But the wonder of good books is that they can faithfully reveal these hidden excellences of human nature and can acquaint us with the inward workings of good hearts and cultured minds. Therefore, in our reading, we may choose our associates from the most excellent of mankind and, through our knowledge of them, learn to emulate their finest characteristics.

Then, too, in our wonderful times, when nations are drawn so much nearer, we can become acquainted with the intellectual and spiritual nobility of all the nations. We should avoid that excessive nationalism which sees no good in people of other nations. On the contrary, we should try to recognize in nationalities, as in individuals, the excellent qualities in which they excel. This is one reason among many why it is a fortunate achievement for anyone to learn a new language. Whenever you learn a new language, you think the thoughts of another race and acquaint yourself with new models to imitate, new excellences to emulate.

Human nature, therefore, lies before you, like a beautiful garden, in which a variety of exquisite flowers delights the eye. Some are more beautiful or more fragrant than others, and through the exercise of your intelligence and your will, choosing from each character its more beautiful blossoms, you can pick for yourself an exquisite bouquet of fine characteristics and make for yourself a personality that will bring color and fragrance into the lives of others.

Chapter Eight

Develop good habits

It would be difficult to enumerate all the various habits that make up that most interesting and important thing which we call character. Under the various circumstances of life, whenever any special opportunity comes to you, or when a temptation assails you, or when you are vexed and worried, you tend to act in a certain characteristic way. This tendency of yours is the result of your personal character.

Those who come in contact with you a great deal study your character instinctively, so that they know beforehand what you are likely to do under certain circumstances. If you are a weak, timid character, they may try to impose on you and to make you give them their way, because they know beforehand that you are apt to yield to them. If you are a strong, determined, stubborn character, they are more cautious with you, because they know you will probably fight back if you are imposed on. If you are a kind, friendly character, they will come to you with confidence, knowing beforehand that you will try to help them. If you are a cold, selfish, unsympathetic character, you are the last one to whom they will bring their troubles, because they know beforehand that you will turn an unsympathetic ear. If you are prompt, energetic, intelligent, and dependable by character, they will instinctively turn to you when they need the help of those qualities.

So, you have something in you that makes you act along certain, definite lines, or inclines you to behave as you have behaved before. Still, you are conscious that you are really free, that while you act in this way, you still could act in another way if you chose. You know that, while you feel the tug and pull of habit, you are yet free to resist it and to build up contrary habits.

For example, if you are very easygoing and self-indulgent by character, when the time comes to get up, you shrink from rising and feel a strong tendency to lie in bed. At the same time, if you are wide awake, you know very well that, if you wish, you can make an effort of the will and throw off this laziness, and that if you do this persistently, morning after morning, you can create in yourself a habit of promptness that will overcome your sloth.

If you are timid and fearful by character, when anything dangerous comes your way, you instinctively shrink and tremble. Still, you know that you are quite free to resist that cowardice and to act in a braver way. If you do this persistently, day after day, you will gain control of your timidity and acquire the habit of courage.

Now, a habit is nothing more or less than an inward tendency to a certain line of action, which springs from the fact that we have often acted in that way in the past, and that we are by nature inclined to do what we have often done before and in the way in which we have done it before.

Every faculty in us, bodily or mental, has this same tendency to form habits. We are a bundle of habits, of many and various kinds. For instance, we have a habit of walking, a habit of carrying ourselves erect or in a stooping position, so that people can recognize us from far off by our stride and posture. We have a habit of taking our food at a certain time, which makes us instinctively grow anxious to eat at that time each day. By maintaining an erect posture for a long time, or by eating at another hour, we can counteract the old habit and form a new one.

Our senses have habits. We habitually listen to some sounds and disregard others. Our mind and our memory are equally subject to habits. Some persons have a habit of attention and concentration, and others, a habit of mental laziness and inattention. The will, in particular, is wonderfully influenced by habits, and these are the most important of our nature, because our will dominates our whole personality.

Our other faculties are not free. The eye cannot help seeing, the ear cannot help hearing, the mind cannot help thinking, the memory cannot help remembering, and the imagination cannot help building up various pictures. But our will can do this or that, can choose good or can choose evil under the appearance of good; it can choose to act or not to act, to obey or to disobey. Our will not only dominates its own decisions, but it has a sway over our whole being. By the continual exercise of willpower, we can make our intellect grow cultured, our imagination fine and pure and active, our memory good, and our whole being more excellent. Day after day, choosing what is good and rejecting what is evil, our will can constantly ennoble our whole personality.

But although our will is free, and remains free, it is still subject, like the rest of our being, to strong habits, which are also the result of its past actions. Every time our will decides, firmly and strongly, it grows in the habit of decision. Every time it wavers foolishly and uselessly, it acquires a greater habit of indecision. Every time we will what is right and good in itself, we increase in the habit of rectitude. Every time we will something that is unworthy in itself, we augment the habit of yielding to evil.

It would take long to enumerate here all our habits, and we shall say more of them later on, but there are four great, fundamental good habits or virtues that are so important and essential that they deserve special mention now. They are the four foundation stones of character, the four deep roots of goodness: prudence, justice, temperance, and fortitude. They are called the cardinal virtues, because the Latin root of *cardinal*, *cardo*, means "hinge," and these virtues are like the four great hinges on which the door of character is firmly hung. To lack any one of them means to have a weak or ignoble character. To possess any one of them to a high degree means to possess all four, for they are linked together in mutual dependence. By studying these four good habits, or virtues, and by cultivating them diligently, we are able to lay the foundation of a strong, good character in a secure and permanent way.

Chapter Nine

Let prudence guide your decisions

Your intellect is the guiding light of your being. It hungers for truth, and it is made to discover and recognize truth, to find new truths from old by combining and comparing them, and to make judgments and form ideas that are true — that is to say, that agree with the world of facts outside of you.

The intellect is like a spiritual mirror, which reflects accurately things presented to it. But it is more than a mirror, because it can reason and arrive at new conclusions correctly, by using what you already know. It is by means of this marvelous faculty that you understand yourself and those around you and that you reflect, learn, and comprehend. It is your reason that directs the actions of your will, by furnishing you with ideas and conclusions as to what is best to do.

Now, prudence, the first of the four great virtues that we have called the foundation stones of character has to do with your intelligence. Prudence is the habit of judging correctly on all occasions what is the right way of acting, so as to fulfill one's duty and attain the rightful end of life. If you look into your own mind, you will see that it is forever working out ways of acting, judging between different courses of conduct, and telling you what it is wise to do under the circumstances.

During your waking hours, you are continually face-to-face with different courses that you may pursue. Sometimes a whole series of possible actions present themselves. For instance, you find yourself face-to-face with a duty, and you can either do it now or postpone it until tomorrow. At the same time, you remember a very attractive amusement that you can patronize instead of doing that insistent duty. A friend comes in at the same moment and asks you, as a special favor, to help him with his work. This makes you remember that there is another task that you ought to perform that is still more insistent than the one you thought of first. The day is only long enough to do one of these four things. Which shall you choose?

Here your intellect considers each one and makes a report to you, so to say, about the relative importance of each. If you have the virtue of prudence — the habit, that is, of judging correctly what is the right way of acting — that intellect of yours will say, "Leave the others aside, and do this one," and it will be right in that suggestion. Then, if your will is conscientious and good, it will follow the right judgment of your intellect, and you will act prudently, discharging your duty as you should and laying up for yourself future satisfaction and reward. But if you lack the virtue of prudence, you will either find great difficulty in deciding at all, or else you may decide wrongly and neglect the thing you ought to have done to choose one of the other, less prudent ways of acting.

If you observe others carefully, you will find that some of them are truly notable for this virtue of prudence in that they can judge quickly and correctly, under most circumstances, what is the best thing to do. Such persons lead reasonable and just lives, and they are good counselors for others.

There are some means of acquiring prudence that you will find extremely practical. One of them is always to take time enough to consider important decisions duly, and to weigh maturely and objectively the reasons for and against any line of conduct.

Suppose, for example, you are face-to-face with a great decision. You already have a good position, let us say, and are getting on well, with fair prospects, but someone suddenly offers you what seems to you a much better position. Should you give up the old position and take up the new? That is a decision that involves serious consequences and is not to be jumped at lightly. A deliberate exercise of prudence is called for. Naturally, your first impulse is to consult those friends of yours in whose judgment you have most confidence and whom you judge to be prudent advisers. Talking the matter over with them and listening to their advice sheds more light on the subject. The motives for and against the change present themselves more and more clearly to your mind. Still you cannot come to a prudent decision. You are still in doubt as to which is better to do: to stay or to go.

You take time to consider. You try to foresee the possible consequences of either mode of action, using your imagination as well as your intelligence to anticipate what will probably happen if you stay in your present position and what will occur if you leave.

You find yourself pulled this way and that by different inclinations. If you are prudent, you try to discount motives that are based mostly on feeling and fancy and to be guided by solid reasons, seeking not what seems most pleasant at the time, but what will really give you the more solid happiness. If you are naturally very fond of money and one of the positions attracts you strongly from that standpoint, you will remind yourself that money is not everything, but that a person is happier where he can be more virtuous, do the more good, and keep his self-respect more surely.

All this careful reflection is an exercise of the virtue of prudence, because by it you are helping yourself to judge correctly and objectively. Finally, you decide and give your answer firmly, realizing that your decision is based on solid reasons and that it is not the result of your impulses or of anybody else's persuasions or of some twist in your makeup that will lead you wrong.

Every time a person exercises the habit of prudence in the way we have mentioned, he grows more prudent, and every time the intellect is thus exerted to judge rightly and carefully as to the best way of acting, it becomes just a little more capable of similar exertion the next time.

Thus, one who grows constantly in prudence will finally become so strengthened in his habit of prudent judgment that he may be depended on to act wisely in varying circumstances. Not only will his own life be happier and more useful in consequence, but those who depend on him and those who consult him about serious questions will find him a tower of strength.

For the sake of others, no less than for your own, you will be wise therefore to cultivate this virtue perseveringly.

Some persons have a great deal of natural prudence, that is, their intellect is naturally inclined to judge rightly and correctly rather than to be influenced by feeling, passions, or prejudices. Other persons are so inclined to act on impulse; they have such a strong imagination and such vivid feelings that they have to make very special efforts to cultivate the virtue of prudence.

Try to weigh your own character, and see toward which group you incline. The criticisms of those who know you will help you in this regard. Ask yourself whether they find you prudent and dependable and whether they naturally come to you for counsel. Then, if you find yourself possessed of a good deal of natural prudence, try to cultivate it by acting on reason and good judgment, by weighing the better method of action, and by looking before you leap in all important enterprises.

Cultivate the habit of remembering the past, so as to see whether you have made errors, and of foresight, so as to be able to look ahead and foresee coming difficulties. It may be interesting to observe, in this connection, that the faults diametrically opposed to prudence are hastiness, thoughtlessness in acting, inconsiderateness, which makes one rush ahead without looking where he is going, changeableness and indecision, taking a resolution and then abandoning it, and wavering between two lines of action in a painful and useless way. On the other hand, a person may have a false prudence by being so cautious that he never makes any decisions, by fretting and worrying over inconsiderable matters, or by being selfishly cautious, crafty, or cunning. These things are as contrary to prudence, through excessive caution, as rashness and negligence are contrary to prudence through lack of judgment. In this, as in all the other virtues, one must hold to the golden middle course and avoid excess as well as deficiency.

Chapter Ten

Practice justice in all its forms

When I say that justice is another of the four foundation stones of character, you will readily agree with me, because no one can be said to have any sort of a good character who is not just. But if I ask you precisely what you mean by *justice*, you may give me various replies. In the very widest sense, justice is almost equivalent to goodness, and, in this sense, when you speak of a just person, you mean one who is good in every regard, and so this word covers the whole of an upright life.

But in speaking of the foundation stones of character, we do not give the word such a wide significance. Here we mean by *justice* that habit of the will which inclines us to give everyone his due, to discharge our duty toward all to whom duty is owed, and to render to everyone what he has a right to receive from us.

Thus *justice* means giving to God due service and honor, giving to our parents filial love and helpfulness, and giving to others what we owe them in the way of service, recompense, and material goods. In other words, to be just is to live up to our obligations toward everyone else.

Recall the last year of your life, and ask yourself, "How far have I been living up to all my duties toward others? And in what regard have I failed to do my full duty toward others?"

These two questions, honestly asked and answered, will go very far toward showing you to exactly what degree you possess the virtue of justice. If you habitually render to others what belongs to them, in the way of service, honor, material goods, truthfulness, and so on through the list of the things we owe to others, you may be thankful that the habit of just dealing is yours to a high degree. Yet you can perfect this habit by constant practice, until you become more and more dutiful, more and more wholehearted in giving to others what you owe them, and more and more just toward God and man.

But if you find by experience that you are continually cutting corners in your work, shirking your duties, defrauding others of what you owe them, even in little things, then you have reason to be very regretful that the virtue of justice is not strongly rooted in your character, and you ought to take all the more care to implant this fine virtue, even at the cost, as need be, of sacrifice, of effort, and of self-discipline. For no one can keep his self-respect unless he is first just toward others.

Let us briefly go over some of the elements of justice, the virtues that group themselves under this great habit.

Truthfulness is a part of justice. We owe it to every person to tell him the truth. Of course, we are not always bound, or even allowed, to tell all the truth, for sometimes we must keep confidences and preserve secrets; but we are not allowed to tell positive untruths to others. When we speak to others, our words should truly express our thoughts. Just as you have a right to the truth from others, so have they from you.

Not only in words but also in actions, a person ought to be honest and sincere. Craftiness, cunning, and slyness are all unjust. And they do you far more harm than they do to others, because they eat at the foundation stone of your character, the habit of justice.

Fidelity and faithfulness to one's promises and engagements is another aspect of the virtue of justice. To be dependable, straightforward, and true to one's word requires a goodly proportion of self-discipline and self-sacrifice. You should neither make promises hastily nor break them easily. These two things often go together. Be slow in giving your word, and sparing of promises, but once you have entered into an agreement, be faithful to it. You owe this to others in justice, and you owe it to yourself. Once one gets the reputation of being slippery and undependable in his agreements and promises, he is done for.

Firmness and strength in resisting evil are also a part of justice. Be kind and gentle, but firm as a rock when there is a question of principle. Good fighters are common enough, and kind, gentle characters are quite frequently found, but when a man is mild, kind, and agreeable, and yet he can stand like a cliff against what he knows to be wrong and evil, he is close to being a perfect character. If you find yourself very much inclined to be easygoing, stiffen your upper lip and straighten your backbone, so that when evil comes, you can stand against it. If you find yourself to be of a hard, unyielding character, make sure that you combine gentleness with strength.

The habit of obeying the law is also an important part of the virtue of justice. Unhappily, respect for the law has diminished considerably in recent times, partly because so many laws have been passed and because some of them have been so unpopular that people dispense themselves from observing them. Remember, though, that the authority of the state comes from God, and it is a sacred thing. When you feel that a law is wrong and unjust, work with all your might to repeal it, but do not ridicule it or get the wrong idea that you are obliged to obey only the laws you like.

It might seem strange to speak of kindness, generosity, and friendliness as part of the virtue of justice, but no man can be entirely just who does not possess these qualities. If we try to measure out to others what strictly belongs to them, without any generosity, without friendliness, we shall surely fall short of the measure we owe them. We all belong to one great human family and therefore are all brothers and sisters; we owe it to each other to be friendly and kind, helpful and generous. The surest way to give to all what is their due is to try to give them a little more than their due.

In all your dealings, therefore, try to be generous, openhanded (with prudence), friendly, and kind. In spite of all the efforts that you make in this direction, you will always find something with which to reproach yourself, because our nature is selfish, self-centered. We have to make strenuous efforts to be generous to and thoughtful of others. Even for the sake of justice, therefore, lean in the direction of unselfishness. The Golden Rule will help you here immensely. If you treat others as you would wish yourself to be treated in like circumstances, you will grow more and more kind, forgiving, and generous, and in so doing, you will grow more and more just.

Finally, gratitude is an important part of justice. We owe it to others to be grateful to them when they have been good to us. It is true that there is no exact measure of gratitude, so one cannot say precisely where we pass the borders of justice in being ungrateful. This is all the more reason, then, for being as grateful as we can.

Chapter Eleven

Be temperate

When we speak of temperance as a foundation stone of character, we do not, of course, mean merely abstaining from drink, which is the sense in which the word is often used. *Temperance* means the habit of self-control and moderation in yielding to bodily appetites. The temperate person will use the good things of the body — food and drink, amusements, and all other corporal things — reasonably.

This habit of self-control and moderation is essential to happiness, and it is absolutely necessary to a virtuous character. The better you get to know yourself, the more you will see that all your faculties tend to make unreasonable demands for gratification. Your mental curiosity is sometimes excessive; your self-esteem is always tending to get out of balance and to demand too much praise and recognition. Your hands are inclined to grasp for more money, and sometimes unreasonably. These impulses have to be controlled and brought under right reason so that you may yield to them only insofar as they are right and proper, and may fight against them insofar as they are wrong and unreasonable.

There is a group of strong impulses over which everyone has to keep a tight rein, as one would handle spirited horses. If you drive these impulses well and control them properly, you can travel fast and far, because they are not wrong in themselves and they can be made good and helpful when properly driven and disciplined. The difference between yielding to them and training them is like the difference between letting a team of horses run wild and driving the same spirited animals skillfully and with control.

Let us consider these impulses a bit, and you will recognize traces of every one of them in your own character.

The first is the craving for esteem, the love of personal excellence. When this exists strongly in one's disposition, it is a spur to effort, a source of power. We speak of one's having a laudable pride in his work, a praiseworthy ambition. As long as this pride and ambition are controlled by temperance and kept within reason, they help a person to get forward, but the virtue of temperance is very necessary to keep them in bounds. As soon as one's ambition becomes unreasonable or his pride excessive, he either grows to be a wretched creature, a burden to himself and to others, or, if he does avoid giving offense, he at least commits faults and errors because of that excessive pride.

The second impulse that requires the control of temperance is the desire we have to get and possess property. It is natural and right for a man to want to make money and have property so as to meet his needs and just obligations. But when this craving for wealth becomes unreasonable and is not kept down by temperance, it grows to be a passion that will lead a man into misery or crime.

Third, there is the craving for pleasure. Pleasure is a good thing in its way, but it has to be moderated by temperance.

Those who go wild after pleasure and fail to exercise reasonable control over their cravings for it become, for want of temperance, miserable and pitiful creatures.

Fourth, consider the impulse of anger. This is a very useful force that gives strength and vigor when a person needs to repel a brutal attack or defend someone who is dear to him. But this impulse of anger, if it is not controlled by temperance and kept within reason, runs away with a person and makes him ridiculous or a dangerous object to society.

Fifth, the craving for food and drink is very strong within us, because food and drink are necessary to existence. But temperance has to step in and regulate the amount of food we take and the amount of drink we allow ourselves (especially when there is a question of strong drink), because these appetites, when indulged excessively, ruin the health and weaken the character.

Sixth, the spirit of emulation, the wish to equal or excel others, is also a healthy impulse when it is reasonable. It urges us on to work and to achieve, but it has to be kept under control also, for, if it degenerates into jealousy and envy, into discontent over the successes of others, it is a curse and a misery.

Finally, we all have a tendency to rest and to take recreation, and this is good and necessary, within bounds. But if that craving for rest grows into laziness and becomes unreasonable — in other words, if it is not tempered by the habitual self-control that the virtue of temperance gives us — then a person becomes lazy, a sluggard, a loafer, or at least a shirker of work that he ought to do.

Every character has some chief or leading fault or evil tendency, which is the taproot of its other defects. Consider these seven basic cravings, and see which one is strongest in you, which one causes you most trouble and brings you most shame and regret. Fix on that one with a particular determination to control it, and you will find that if you overcome that leading tendency in your disposition, you will master all the others and acquire the virtue of temperance.

There is no way to get this virtue except by practice, by deliberately exercising yourself in self-denial, self-control, and self-discipline, by acting against the impulses in your nature that you see are too strong and unruly, unreasonable and excessive.

Begin now. Practice temperance virtuously, and you will lay the foundation for a strong character and a happy life.

Chapter Twelve

Develop fortitude

The fourth foundation stone of character — the virtue of fortitude — stands out most clearly in the virtuous character. Fortitude is that good habit by which a person courageously undertakes labors and faces dangers when duty calls, or conscience speaks, or when there is some worthy end to be attained. Fortitude is more than courage and more than bravery, although it includes these virtues. A courageous person can face danger, but he cannot always sustain labors and bear weariness and disappointment to gain his end. Patience, as well as courage, is a part of fortitude, and one who is really endowed with this virtue to a high degree can bear disappointments, delays, and weariness with unfaltering perseverance, just as he can face dangers and hardships for the sake of attaining the good end he has set out to reach.

The poet Horace, in one of his odes, draws a magnificent picture of a strong man, tenacious of his purpose, of whom he says that if the whole universe should crash around him in shattering fragments, the ruins would strike him down indeed, but they would strike him down still undismayed.[5] History is

[5] Cf. Horace, *Odes*, Bk. 3, no. 3, line 7.

full of examples of fortitude, and the heroes of all nations have shone by this trait.

The greatest of all historical examples of fortitude is, of course, the example of Christ, whose whole life was an exercise of this virtue, as it was of prudence, justice, and temperance. He combined the summit of bravery with the perfection of gentleness. The threats of His enemies never deterred Him, and He bore the death of the Cross without flinching.

The history of early Rome is full of examples of fortitude, half legend and half history. Consider Quinctius Curtius, leaping fully armed into the chasm in the earth to appease the wrath of the gods, and Mutius Scaevola, calmly placing his hand in the fire to show the enemies of Rome what manner of men they had to deal with. These ancient Romans are legendary examples of fortitude.

The history of the Jewish people is rich in instances of fortitude. Recall the heroism of the prophets, who spoke the truth in the face of popular clamor and hatred and withstood the persecution of wicked kings, and the patient courage of the warriors who defended Israel against its enemies. Consider the intrepidity of men like Tobias, who risked death to give the dead a becoming burial;[6] the bravery of women like Judith, who single-handedly slew Holofernes in his tent and delivered Israel from destruction;[7] and the boldness of Esther, who went unsummoned before King Assuerus to plead for her people.[8] Remember the fortitude of Job, whose spirit no sufferings

[6] Cf. Tob. 2:8.

[7] Jth. 13:9-10.

[8] Cf. Esther 15:9 ff.

could crush, the manly bravery of David, and, in later times, the martyr spirit of the Maccabees. These are all glorious models of the virtue of fortitude.

American history has many instances of fortitude. George Washington had this virtue to a high degree, calmly continuing the desperate war for liberty, with a heart full of sorrow for the suffering of his soldiers, harassed by many foes, yet firmly continuing until he won the victory of freedom. In pictures of him, the artist Gilbert Stuart has well brought out his characteristic virtue of fortitude in the calm set of his lips, the steadfast composure of his face.

When we look on the pictures of Abraham Lincoln, his brave, sad face is full of fortitude. It is he who bore on his shoulders the weight of that heartrending struggle in which half of our nation hurled itself against the other in desperate conflict. He truly loved his native land, and he needed the stuff of which heroes are made to keep him firm in that hour of terrible trial when every battle was won by the spilling of the blood of brothers and when victory could come only through the defeat of part of his nation.

You may never have to face such trials as these men endured, but in your own way, you need the virtue of fortitude as much as they did. Bring yourself to account and see whether you possess this virtue in its fullness. Do you have courage to face danger for the sake of principle? Can you stand up before a crowd and calmly maintain your point where you feel it is your duty? Do you also possess the patience to bear delays and to persevere to the end, until you achieve what you have proposed to accomplish? Can you go through weariness and disappointment without being discouraged or faltering? Are you able to bear even with yourself and your own weaknesses in order to succeed and to serve others well?

If you lack any of these elements of fortitude, face that lack frankly and begin doing the very things that you find difficult in this matter of fortitude. You can build up and round out your character by constant practice. When you feel like compromising or surrendering, then is the time to stiffen the fibers of your will and to determine not to yield. Little by little, day by day, inch by inch, you can approach the summit of fortitude. Every struggle is an honor to you, just as it is a supreme disgrace to yield and be a coward.

A companion virtue of fortitude is the splendid quality of great-mindedness, or magnanimity, which makes a person desire to achieve noble and honorable deeds. A great-minded person is exalted in his ambitions, high in his views. He will not stoop to mean, petty ends or merely selfish purposes. He is a public-spirited citizen, a generous friend, and a helpful member of society. Such people benefit the whole circle in which they move. They are never satisfied with half-achievements, mediocre work, or imperfect equipment for their task. Great-mindedness is the fine flower of fortitude, because to be great-minded requires courage to pursue and patience to bear until one's high ambition is attained.

Another companion virtue of fortitude is constancy and tenacity of purpose, which carries a person on through every difficulty, danger, and delay until he gains his worthy end. No one ever deserved the praise of fortitude unless he had the courage to carry on in the face of difficulty. Washington, at Valley Forge, reviewing his destitute army; Lincoln, in the White House, waiting for the tidings of war: these men now seem of heroic stature to us, but to themselves they were but weak human beings, buffeted by a tide of misfortunes, struggling on, day after day, in the face of such discouragement and weariness that it took immense constancy of purpose to enable them to stand their ground.

In your own struggles and difficulties, you will need the same virtue, although perhaps not to such a great degree. Carry on, whatever may come. Put one foot before the other, struggling forward with determined constancy, and you will be able to achieve any project. But if you lack this heroic virtue, nothing you do will be of any permanent value. You will begin and not have the constancy to finish. You will be discouraged by slight obstacles and will give up the fight just, perhaps, when victory is coming over the hill.

Notice that while fortitude keeps the golden middle way, the two vices that are opposed to it are cowardice and rashness. Cowardice destroys fortitude by undermining one's courage so that he becomes timid and fearful. Rashness is an excess of daring, which takes away one's reasonable and prudent caution. A rash person is no more possessed of fortitude than a coward is.

You can readily see that all four foundation stones of character depend on one another. One cannot have real fortitude unless he is prudent, just, and temperate. You cannot conceive of a truly just person unless, at the same time, he is possessed of prudence, temperance, and fortitude. Prudence will tell him when and how to practice justice. Temperance will enable him to subdue his excessive desires and impulses, which would otherwise lead him into injustice and oppression; temperance will give him the courage and patience to render to everyone what is his own. So, also, in order to be temperate, one must be just, giving everyone his own; one must be prudent, weighing well the right way of acting; and one must have fortitude enough to control and subdue his own instincts when they would drag him into excesses.

Thus, all these virtues, with a faithful balance, depend on one another, and if you succeed in cultivating any one of them to a notable degree, you will possess them all, and your character will be firmly set and strongly balanced on these foundation stones of a worthy character and a noble life.

Chapter Thirteen

Choose happiness over pleasure

It may seem a strange thing to say, but often in your life you will have to choose between pleasure and happiness. You will be forced to decide, of your own free will, whether you will make wrongful pleasure a principal purpose in your life and thereby inevitably forfeit happiness, or whether you will deliberately choose to give up the pursuit of unlawful pleasure and, in so doing, become happy.

As you go on in life, you will see more and more the truth of this observation, which is profoundly rooted in human nature. You will see the difference between pleasure and happiness, and you will observe that professional pleasure-seekers are never happy. On the other hand, the truly happy people are those who have schooled themselves deliberately to give up some pleasures.

Let us reflect for a minute on the practical meaning of pleasure and of happiness.

Pleasure means enjoyment. It means the gratifying of some sense or faculty in which we take delight. Every one of our human faculties, whether of body or of soul, has its own particular craving. Our eyes are constantly longing to look and to see things that are beautiful, interesting, or agreeable.

Our appetite for food is constantly craving the satisfaction of eating and drinking. Our muscles crave exercise.

Even our mind, memory, and imagination crave the gratification of their own particular faculty. The mind wants to know more and more, and it derives pleasure from learning, from hearing news, and from discussing and debating. The imagination craves amusements, stories, plays, movies, and pleasurable reading of every kind.

Such craving for pleasure is especially intense in our day, because there are so many things that stir it up, and so many means of gratifying this thirst for pleasure. In older, simpler times, people had to work hard for very little. Their food was simple, and children nowadays would probably look down on their amusements. They had no cars, no movies, no airplanes, no dance halls, and no such variety of amusing magazines and newspapers. They probably enjoyed life as much as or more than people do today, but they were not stimulated so much and stirred up to seek all manner of amusements, and they did not have nearly so many ways of gratifying their thirst for pleasure.

Then, too, modern methods of advertising are continually urging people to satisfy their craving for pleasure and are developing new wants that are profitable to satisfy. Notice the advertisements on billboards for a single day, and observe how many of them are given over to creating or stimulating your desire for pleasure. You are invited to smoke, to eat candy, to chew gum, to go to the movies, to read magazines and books that are principally pleasure-giving, or to have a good time in general. Consciously or unconsciously, you react to these incitements. The power of suggestion is immense, and you are constantly being tempted by suggestions to do things for the pleasure of doing them — things not wrong in themselves, perhaps, but which take just so much of your energy, your time, and your means.

Let us get this whole subject straight in our minds. Pleasure in itself is a good thing, and a certain amount of lawful pleasure is necessary for us. We need a certain amount of exercise and a certain amount of amusement, just as we need a certain amount of sleep and of food. The need for pleasure is not so absolute as the need for food, but it is still very real. The pity is, however, that we are so constituted that we never get enough pleasure; pleasure always leaves us unsatisfied and begets a desire for more. Therefore, the temptation of our day is to pursue pleasure for its own sake, which means to neglect duty for the sake of pleasure.

Those who seek pleasure for its own sake are somewhat like people who take drugs. At first, they experience some gratification, but after a while, they take the drug simply to satisfy a terrible craving. They are no happier with the drug than they once were without it. On the contrary, they are far more unhappy now, because the drug is gradually undermining their whole nervous system. But they keep on taking larger and larger doses, simply to keep themselves going, until their constitution breaks down.

Pleasure is not a drug. It is a very useful thing in itself when employed as a means to an end. But when it is taken in excessive doses, for its own sake, it takes on some of the characteristics of a drug. Pleasure-seekers sacrifice more and more for the sake of pleasure, and, in the end, they find themselves broken down in character and sometimes broken down in health, and essentially unhappy, because they are essentially dissatisfied. The only thing that will keep them going is more pleasure, and pleasure itself has palled on them.

Such is pleasure, but what is happiness?

Happiness, as we understand it, is the inward contentment, the peace and satisfaction, the moral well-being that comes to a person of prudence, justice, temperance, and fortitude, who does his work and discharges his duty to God and his fellowmen with patience, fidelity, uprightness, and kindness. Pleasure is merely the passing gratification of some faculty. One may get pleasure by eating and drinking, by going to a show, by reading an interesting book, or by engaging in sports, but happiness is a lasting state of inward contentment.

Just as health of body requires a balance of the faculties — so that a person experiences a general sense of physical well-being — so happiness comes from health of soul and mind and heart. It results from a balance of moral qualities. A person cannot be happy if he has a bad conscience, lacks self-respect, or is aware that he is shirking his duty toward God and man.

Hence, happiness of mind and soul, like health of body, must be secured by a balance of our faculties, by keeping in a state of spirit that will enable us to be happy. It is easy, then, to see the real conflict that exists between following pleasure for its own sake and seeking happiness.

We are so constituted that, if a person deliberately seeks pleasure for its own sake, he is sure to neglect his duty, and this is true even of innocent pleasure. The time that he ought to give to work is stolen for pleasure. The effort and ambition that he ought to devote to doing his duty is spent in pleasure-seeking. If this is true even of innocent pleasures, it is tenfold true of pleasures that are wrong. To seek these in any degree is ruinous, because a man thereby loses his self-respect, neglects his duty, and goes directly against the requirements we have laid down for happiness.

But even as regards innocent pleasures, you have to choose between using them moderately and with self-control and seeking happiness, or seeking them for their own sake and inevitably ceasing to be happy. This is a distinction of such tremendous importance that no one can calculate how many lives are ruined and how much is sacrificed by its neglect. You are quite free to choose one or the other, but choose you must. If you seek pleasure for its own sake, you cannot be happy. If you wish to be truly happy, then, you must moderate and control your thirst for pleasure.

Chapter Fourteen

Learn to do without nonessentials

It is a curious fact that what you leave undone is sometimes as important for your success as what you do. What you are willing to give up has as much influence on your character as what you are willing to do. There is no use in trying to deceive yourself on this point. To secure the things essential for success, you have to give up much that is nonessential, and to buy what is excellent, you have to forgo much that is good.

Many lack the wisdom of knowing what to give up. They try to grasp at everything, and they catch nothing. They try to hold on to many unimportant objects of desire, and they lose the most important ones.

For example, a young man will start out with the firm resolve of making a success in a profession. The way to professional success is study and practice, and the young man starts out with a real purpose of study, and he begins well. But in a very short time, amusements present themselves, friendships thicken, and a bit of romance enters into his experience. These things make demands on his energy, time, and attention, and these demands are antagonistic to study.

If our young man has the wisdom to know how to give up nonessentials, he will calmly stick to his books, saying to himself that these other things are very pleasant and good in their way, but he cannot use his time and energy on other objects and still hope to study and succeed in his profession. So he cuts down his time spent on amusements to what is really necessary, he makes his appointments with his friends secondary to his appointments with his books, and he keeps himself in good form for serious mental application, which carries him along through his studies and lays the foundation for a successful professional career. This young man knows how and what to give up, and his future success is going to be directly in proportion to his present capacity to judge what to leave undone and what to do.

The temptation is very great nowadays to multiply occupations, amusements, and sidelines, and if a person does not know what to give up, one of two things is pretty sure to follow. Either he will neglect his main business in life and do his work poorly because he takes on so many other occupations, or else he will exhaust that reserve of energy which is limited in each individual, and so he will break down in health, or at least lose efficiency. You ought to make a study of yourself, your surroundings, and your opportunities, and decide what to quit, what to cut down on, and what to cut out altogether. Anyone who has not the good sense and the courage to do this runs the risk of becoming one of those unfortunate persons who do nothing well and never finish what they begin, because they do not know what to give up.

You can apply this principle profitably in every department of life. Take the matter of reading, for example. The man who wishes for real success in life ought to cultivate his mind by planned reading. Develop this habit, and you will find it just as pleasant and much more profitable than the habit of browsing here and there in magazines and newspapers, without any definite purpose. Planned reading, along chosen lines, will do more for your mind in a month than will years of mere mental dissipation. But a large part of the practice of good reading depends on the wisdom and willpower to be able to give up the sort of reading that perhaps you like the best.

Of ten men who resolve to read according to a plan, only one, perhaps, succeeds. The others wish to read worthwhile books, but it is only a wish. They cannot give up the desultory reading that takes up their time. They must devour the newspapers and read magazines and fiction, so all the time they have during the day to read is wasted.

The same principle may well be applied in your amusements. Keeping away from cheap, worthless amusements and, still more, from evil ones is a necessary condition for frequenting good ones. Everyone nowadays has to choose from a multitude of possible occupations for his evenings and holidays. Amusing the public has grown to be a huge business, well advertised and well organized, and you have to fight against the attraction and appeal of a dozen cheap and indifferent amusements in order to set your feet on the way that leads to a good, helpful, and improving one. Unfortunately, the majority of humankind is a great deal like sheep. They follow witless leaders, and so they throng to entertainments and amusements that have but little substance in them and that leave the mind weaker and the body less fit than before. To choose the right amusements means to give up the indifferent ones.

The same thing is true of friendships and associates. To make the right sort of friends, one has to keep away from the wrong sort. Many, through mere weakness, consort with those whom they know to be unworthy of anyone's friendship, and this folly has two bad consequences for them: they find their own good manners corrupted, and they find that decent and worthy friends avoid them. The ability to give up these unworthy associates is essential to the ability to make worthy friends, which are surely one of man's greatest treasures.

Recall your recent experiences, and try to calculate how far you possess this extremely precious faculty of being able to give up and surrender the nonessential things for the sake of essential ones. Exercise yourself every now and then by deliberately sacrificing something that you have no real reason to keep and that stands in the way of true achievement. If you exercise your intelligence in deciding what you ought to give up, you will, in carrying out those decisions, grow in the ability of judicious surrender. It will be one of the most precious and practical of your achievements in character building.

Chapter Fifteen

Be pleasant in your demeanor and in your actions

A pleasant manner is one that appeals to others, charms them, and makes them like you. A pleasant character is one that is agreeable to others. When a person is of a pleasant disposition, everyone is glad to have him around. Faces light up at his approach. His friendship is sought and his company is appreciated, because everyone likes to be pleased and dislikes, naturally, to be displeased.

Throughout life, you will be constantly in contact with other people. You have to deal with them, influence them, associate with them, work for them, or direct them. Now, if you go to the trouble of cultivating all the pleasant elements in your personality, the result will be that your life will flow more smoothly, and you will be able to do your work far, far better. Your contacts with other people will be frictionless, where an unpleasant character and disposition would continually grate on them. Many otherwise very good people lead a miserable existence and make others miserable as well, because they do not have the virtue of pleasantness. And, unfortunately, many rascals get on in the world and make many friends because they have pleasant dispositions.

Your own interests, and the interests of others, ought to induce you to try to be pleasant always and everywhere. Your own interests should induce you, because pleasantness will be for you like oil on troubled waters, making your passage through life much easier. For the sake of others, also, you ought to try to be pleasant, because this quality in you will spread sunshine and kind feelings everywhere, while an unpleasant and disagreeable manner will cause you to be a source of trouble and gloom, irritation and distress.

Try to be pleasant always and everywhere. There are some persons who are extremely obliging and kind and agreeable when they are out in company, but who take no trouble at all to be pleasant at home. They are, according to the old saying, home devils and social angels. This is a kind of hypocrisy that honorable people ought to detest, because if you are not pleasant and kind at home, your kind behavior in society is only a costume that you put on for the occasion. The same thing may be said about those who are pleasant with some groups and disagreeable with others, who are agreeable to the rich, the important, and the influential, and behave disagreeably to those who, as they think, can do them little good or cause them little harm.

What are the elements of pleasantness? It begins in a person's interior and requires that he be kind, solicitous for the interests of others, and sympathetic with their feelings. It demands an unselfish attitude, the willingness to oblige, and a wish to please. This inward disposition is required to be truly pleasant, because, otherwise, outward pleasantness would be only a sort of play-acting, by which we would assume a character that is not really ours.

If you wish to be pleasant, therefore, get into the habit of judging kindly of others and thinking well of all they do, be interested in their concerns, and feel for their sorrows and their successes. This will not only tend to make your exterior pleasant, but it will make you cheerful also. When you think of the interest of others, when you rejoice with their joys and sorrow with their sorrows, you are really getting rid of your own burdens.

Moreover, thoughts have a way of showing themselves in one's exterior. If you are interiorly happy and charitable, kind and sympathetic, your face will naturally tend to become agreeable, cheerful, and pleasing, and your actions will reflect the interior glow of kindness. Do not, for pity's sake, try to force a pleasant appearance and agreeable manner, but let them glow naturally from an inward gentleness and courtesy of thought.

There are two sides to every character, the light and the dark side, and you may choose which one to look upon in others. If you seek out the defects and misdeeds of others, you can find them very easily. We all have enough faults, but if you accustom yourself to look on the good qualities of those around you and to excuse their human imperfections, you will get to like them better. This is the way you wish others to treat you; you want them to give you credit for all the good that is in you and to excuse all the imperfection and evil. By following the Golden Rule, therefore, you will give yourself the great advantage of a kindly outlook on human nature.

But all this inward kindness and amiability will be lost on other people unless you express it by your outward actions. Mind readers are extremely rare (if indeed they exist at all), and so everyone is obliged to read everyone else's mind and disposition by his looks, his actions, and his words. Some people have faces suited for the expression of pleasant, kind thoughts. Some people's faces are naturally solemn and expressionless. Civilized folk usually wear a somewhat neutral expression like a mask, to cover their feelings.

Spend one day in the midst of a gloomy, solemn-looking, expressionless multitude of people, and you will find yourself intensely depressed. Pass another day in the midst of a pleasant, smiling group, and see how cheerful you become in consequence. You affect others just as they affect you. So let your face light up now and then with a smile, with a kind look, and indicate to others by your expression the inward geniality and kindness that they will so much appreciate.

Tones of voice also have a great deal to do with pleasantness. People judge by your inflections as much as by your words, and there are some people who lift up the heart of the hearer by the mere tones of their voices — cheerful, kindly, helpful tones.

Courtesy and good manners are likewise very important parts of a pleasant personality. It requires a good deal of self-discipline, observation, and effort to acquire really beautiful manners, which are not obtrusive and yet are perfect in their poise and charm.

The substance of your speech is, of course, all important when it comes to being pleasant to others. Caustic wit, sarcastic or unfeeling jests, and harsh criticism do not go with a pleasant character. Those who allow themselves to become uncharitable in speech, who backbite others, or who repeat evil rumors may hurt themselves even more than they hurt the object of their evil speech. They ruin the pleasantness of their own character, and even if their hearers do not believe what they say against others, they retain the impression of a caustic, sour, unpleasant personality.

Many of the elements of a pleasant personality will come up for consideration later, because pleasantness is a harmony of many strings, and to be pleasant, one has to attend to various details of action, speech, and conduct. But it is worthy to deal seriously with oneself on this subject and to ask oneself, "In what degree do I possess the excellent and magical quality of pleasantness to others, and how may I improve and perfect such a lovely and efficacious quality of character?"

Chapter Sixteen

Develop your power of observation

There is a vast difference between seeing and observing. A hundred men may see the same event, read the same book, or meet the same person, and every one of the hundred will observe in a different way and perceive different details. What we see merely passes across the mirror of our eyes. What we observe is noted, grasped, and stored up in our mind. You will find that you can wonderfully cultivate this faculty of observation by attention and effort.

By nature, people have varying degrees of this power. Some are born with a keen, observing eye. They naturally tend to take in details, to comprehend and retain impressions. Others are not at all gifted in this regard. They are by nature dreamy, unobservant. Things pass before their eyes like shadows and leave very little impression on their memory and imagination. One who is gifted with keen observation needs to discipline it and direct it. One who has very little power to observe needs all the more to train himself in careful and retentive observation.

It is curious, too, that people are selective in their observation, and you must be selective to a certain extent, if you wish to succeed in your chosen task. Thus, a doctor may be very unobservant of some things, but he must have a very keen and accurate power of seeing and recognizing the physical symptoms of disease. All his senses help him to take note of the small and sometimes very obscure signs by which one disease can be distinguished from another.

The lawyer has to be observant of the moral and mental characteristics of others. He has to be a good judge of character, which is the result of the trained power of observation. He must be able to see the points in a legal document, to observe and retain the leading features of decisions. It is quite evident that the trained power of observation of the doctor is quite different in its exercise from the same faculty in a lawyer.

Businessmen, in order to succeed, need to cultivate their powers of observation. A shrewd buyer is a man who has observed carefully the different grades of material and knows how to associate with each the price that should be asked for it. Different businesses and professions require different knowledge and different kinds of observation. But it is this power of observation that puts people into contact with the facts, and it is only by reasoning from facts and acting upon facts that true success is obtainable in any profession or business.

In any career, then, the power of observation is very important. But if you take up literature or journalism in any of their forms, you need a particular skill in observing. The world is spread out before you, various and wonderful. The material for stories, news, and poems is rich and plentiful.

The journalist is not concerned with literature as such; he reports faithfully the news of the day. But even here it is evident enough that observation is necessary. Some people have what is called an eye for news. They can distinguish, in an instant, what will be of interest to readers and what will not. They can seize on the salient points of an event and write it up effectively. Sometimes this is largely a natural gift, but it may also be cultivated, and the really successful journalist is one who will go to the trouble of observing and weighing the various items that come to his attention, so as to make more and more effective his power of observation.

It is related of a famous magician that he trained himself systematically for years in alertness of eye and retentive memory. One of the means he used was this: he would walk swiftly past a shop window in which a number of objects were contained, and, as he passed, he would take one rapid glance at the array of various articles. Then he would try to recall as many of the things he had looked at as he could. At first, his glance took in the whole window, but really only observed three or four articles. Little by little, through practice, he came to see more and more objects, until at last he could, after one glance, mention several dozen different things that he had seen in his swift inspection of the window.

He used this alertness of observation in a trick. A closed box, in which a number of objects had been placed beforehand, of which he had no knowledge, was presented to him on stage. He would hold the box for a moment in full view of the audience and then describe the unseen objects within the box, amid general astonishment. The explanation of the trick was that, with lightning-like quickness, he could whip off the cover of the box and put it back again so rapidly that the untrained eye of the audience could not perceive the movement. But his trained eye, in that instant, could observe all the contents of the box.

In this matter, as in everything else, you will find that real success comes from hard work. No matter how much of the natural gift of observation a man possesses, he has to make some effort and go to some trouble to train that power. Those who, by nature, possess very little of the faculty of observation can, by self-discipline and effort, become very expert, at least, along the particular lines that their lifework requires. It is rather a good plan in this connection to take up some study, or some amusement even, that requires the exercise of observation. The natural sciences, such as botany, zoology, and the study of insects, all help to cultivate one's power of observation, because they make him notice minute differences and classify similar objects according to their variations.

The same thing may be said about descriptive writing. If a man keeps a notebook by him and jots down the characteristic features of the places he visits, he will grow notably in the power of observation by exercising that faculty. To associate with people with highly trained powers of observation is also a very good means of developing this faculty. If you take a stroll with an expert botanist, you will be amazed to see how many varieties of plants and flowers he can show you, even in a neighborhood where you have lived for years. The reading of books that manifest high powers of observation is also a help in self-training.

You will find it interesting and pleasant to cultivate your powers of observation. We all have the natural and laudable curiosity to know more and more about the world in which we live and the people with whom we associate. The mere reading of books will never put you in the possession of such vivid and actual knowledge as will your own native powers of observation. Like all other faculties, this one gives pleasure by its mere exercise. Besides, it opens up greater and greater avenues of service, for it remains true that a man is useful and helpful in direct proportion to his definite and particular knowledge, the fruit of observation.

Chapter Seventeen

Be yourself

The wise Creator of mankind made us all just a little different, and it is our differences and not our similarities that make us interesting.

The great benefactors of mankind and the geniuses who enriched human nature and history have always been brave enough to be different from their fellows, and it was by their differences that they conferred a benefit on the human race. You may not be a genius, since these are rare, and you may never be able to put humanity into your debt by your achievements, but you have a little circle of friends and acquaintances who depend a great deal upon you for their entertainment and cheer and for help in other ways.

It is by being brave enough to be individual and by cultivating your agreeable differences from others that you can help them. Tendencies, talents, and preferences all differ extraordinarily in different individuals. If you yield to bashfulness and timidity and insist upon being like everyone else, the nice individuating tones in your character, the points in which you are capable of being interesting and helpful, will be, in great part, lost, and you will become a humdrum sort of person, uninteresting and unhelpful.

Is it not refreshing to meet a man or woman who is a real individual with personal enthusiasms and personal talents and characteristics? Just as you look on others, so they look on you. You have some special talent in you. It may be for music, for art, or perhaps for entertaining or public speaking; perhaps it is a mechanical ingenuity that devises amusements for others. Whatever this talent of yours may be, get it out and have a look at it, and see whether you are using it to the utmost. Not for your own benefit only, but for the benefit of others as well, that little talent of yours ought to be kept in active working order and to be trotted out on occasion without bashfulness or undue timidity.

People may become humdrum and monotonous because there is such a strong tendency in the modern world to be standardized and conformed to fashions and customs. Everyone has to think the same ideas, to hold the same opinions, to wear the same sort of clothes, to read the same magazines and books. Individuality and spontaneous freshness are pushed out by this sort of uniformity.

Notice that this very monotony puts differences at a premium. When people look for a place to visit, they choose their destination because it has something to recommend it that other places have not. It may be the scenery, some special amusements or sports, or the climate. It is not the sameness of the city that attracts visitors, but its individual and pleasant differences. Some cities are beginning to realize this and are deliberately making themselves different by establishing special attractions, or cultivating a special style of architecture, or doing some other thing to make it worthwhile to go there rather than anywhere else.

It is the same way with individuals. People are continually looking not for mediocre, average, commonplace, individuals, but for those who have some difference, some individuality, some special talent or power. Those who are responsible for great businesses complain that one of their chief difficulties is to find good executives, those who stand out for their individual capacity and power to bear responsibility. It has always been true in the professions as in business that there is plenty of room at the top. The person who is different from his fellows, more highly qualified, more expert and skillful, has always found ample opportunities.

This is eminently true nowadays for several reasons. One is that the standardized education of today, with its tendency to reduce everybody to a common level, has resulted in an epidemic of mediocrity in which specially qualified people are relatively rare. Another reason is that the vast multiplication of opportunities and the resulting needs for leadership have made it necessary to find a larger number of highly qualified workers than before.

For both these reasons, you will be wise if you deliberately cultivate your individual differences. Be yourself, and do not allow the fear of ridicule or your natural bashfulness or timidity or any other deterring influence to keep you from being yourself. God made you with some special talents, capacities, powers, interests, and good inclinations. By judiciously cultivating these, you will make yourself agreeable and efficient, and you will find that place in the world of men and of affairs which you are specially qualified to fill.

Chapter Eighteen

Discipline your imagination

Among your faculties there is one that, unless it is disciplined and kept in control, is apt to do more to make a fool of you and lead you wrong than any other. It was Nicolas Malebranche, the French thinker, who coined the phrase "the fool of the house" to describe the imagination.

During all your waking hours, pictures are forming themselves in your imagination, whether you are conscious of them or not. Your memory recalls past scenes as they were. But the imagination comes into play and changes those former scenes and experiences into new shapes. When you daydream, for example, you see yourself in new surroundings, you are the hero of remarkable adventures and achievements that never were or will be, and you pass through admiring throngs and are hailed as heroes are hailed. Things that never happened and never will happen may thus become more real to you than reality itself, so that you may fall into such a deep reverie as not to notice what goes on around you.

This picturing faculty is nearly as spontaneous and constant as thought itself. It runs along with the workings of your intelligence, so that as soon as you think of something, the imagination tries to body forth that thought in an image. You think of a fortune, and your imagination conjures up a vision of gold and jewels. You think of courage, and your imagination represents the battlefield, with yourself, perhaps, as a hero, taking and giving wounds. You think of rest, and your imagination pictures a still lake and a shady seat on the shore, under the trees. You think of home, and your imagination gives you a picture of it, with your mother moving about at her daily tasks or your brothers and sisters gathered around the family table.

The imagination is continually running forward into the future, trying to conjecture what will happen in days to come. It anticipates pleasures and pains. You think of going on a journey, and your imagination shows you whirling along in a car, or perhaps it will take a sudden twist and represent a terrible accident, in which you are writhing under the ruins of a burning train. Sometimes this imagination of yours deceives you by picturing future joys and satisfactions that never will come to pass. You dream of riches, happiness, and contentment that may come if you take some special step, such as if you give up your present position and go to another one. These dreams are much brighter than the reality would be, and your imagination presents them so vividly that they may induce you to take a foolish step, to give up what you have in order to grasp at something you never will get.

Or, you have to face a difficult duty, and you naturally shrink from it. Your imagination adds to your difficulty by suddenly bringing up a fanciful picture of far greater obstacles and impediments than really exist.

That is why Malebranche said that the imagination is the fool of the house, because it plays so many tricks on us and works on our feelings so unreasonably by its changes of view and vision. It is like a perpetual movie, running across the screen of our consciousness, casting now comedies, now tragedies, now the true and accurate reflection of reality, now a mere made-up picture of never-to-be-realized things.

But while your imagination may thus play the fool with you and thus make a fool of you unless you correct it and discipline it, still it can also be of sublime service. It is the imagination that helps to give interest to character. It also confers the ability to see big projects and follow them through in your mind, by foreseeing the difficulties and the ways to success.

The trained imagination of the poet and the artist sweep through heaven and earth to find forms of beauty and of power. By its aid they create wonderful poems and masterpieces of painting and sculpture. The inward eye of the imagination sees these beautiful visions vividly, before they are expressed in words or delineated in colors or carved in marble. The splendors of human architecture, as well as the wonders of human machinery, are the result, to a large degree, of the creative imagination.

You can profit by these reflections to stir yourself up to a real zeal for the cultivation of your imagination. It is a wonderful servant, but a tyrannical master. People who train and enrich their imaginations by study and observation, discipline and self-control, acquire a power over their fellows and a grasp of the truth that fits them for the service of God and man.

Those who allow their imagination to run riot with them find it indeed to be the fool of the house, forever upsetting their plans, disturbing their calculations, stirring them to vain fears, or bearing them up with foolish and wind-blown hopes. The imagination must be brought under the dominion of the reason and the will. When the imagination aids the reason and the will, and is obedient to them and in accord with their decisions, then it is good and helpful. When it grows unreasonable, it ought to be disciplined like a foolish child.

It is useful for you to observe how much you are influenced by your imagination. When vain fears rise up to scare you, bring them to the test of reason, and force your imagination to come within bounds. When extravagant hopes and expectations turn your head, come to the solid earth, and try to see things as they really are, so as not to be misled. This continual discipline of the imagination will curb its tendency to play the fool with you.

You should also discipline and cultivate your imagination by reading good literature. Fine, worthy, imaginative literature enriches and ennobles your imagination by feeding it with true images and beautiful fancies. Great poetry, great drama, and great fiction, therefore, nourish the imagination.

Be extremely careful, however, what food you give this mighty faculty. The tainted, seductive, licentious fiction of today is a poison to it, and once the imagination is filled with unworthy and vile images, cleansing it becomes a herculean task. Indeed, it never does give up the wickedness that you throw into its retentive pool.

The pictures that this tainted fiction evokes in the reader are of a sordid, false, and morbid nature. They seem, as one reads, to be merely passing impressions. But science assures us that what goes into the imagination is never lost and never passes away. Thus, a person may seem to forget these morbid images, but at some future hour, when the person least thinks it, they may start up again into the consciousness, and the imagination will then take bitter revenge for the insults offered it in the past.

It is far, far better to look on your imagination as something sacred and excellent, and carefully preserve it from pollution. Fill it with noble, worthy, strong, pure images from great art, good literature, the conversation of worthy men, and the contemplation of God's beautiful world and of the finer aspects of humanity. Discipline it, and insist that it dwell on what is excellent, beautiful, and elevating.

Then your imagination will be no longer the fool of the house, a fickle and deceptive faculty. It will be, on the contrary, a strong helper to the intellect, a powerful aid in creative work, along the lines of your profession or calling. It will be a handmaid to literature and a comfort and a source of keenest pleasure in writing and conversation, in your leisure reflections and in your quiet thoughts.

Chapter Nineteen

Strengthen your will

You are conscious that you are free, and, even in spite of yourself, you must act on that conviction. Just what this freedom means, you may never have reflected, and you may find it difficult to define. You may reason about it and grow very much perplexed in determining in just what it consists. But when you are confronted with the alternative of doing good or of doing evil, and when you find yourself hesitating between two courses of action, both of which appear to you desirable, then you are conscious that you are free to choose. You are aware that you can determine your own choice, and, although others can influence you, or persuade you, or offer you reasons for acting one way or the other, still, finally, the determination rests within you.

When you do wrong, you feel sorry, because you know that the wrong has been deliberate and intentional. When you do a good deed, you feel a glow of satisfaction, because you know that you deserve credit for freely doing what is right. In matters where your power of choice does not enter in, and where you cannot help acting as you do, you feel no satisfaction when the thing is good, nor any self-accusation when it is evil.

Thus, if you were to trip on the carpet and involuntarily jolt someone else and cause him to fall and be hurt, if your stumbling were involuntary, you would feel regret, but no sense of guilt. You would be sorry that the accident had happened, but would say frankly that it was not your fault. But if you deliberately pushed someone, in anger, and caused him the same injury, you would feel a deep sense of guilt afterward, because you had freely chosen to do a wicked thing.

Now, this power of choosing one thing when you are free to choose another, of doing this rather than that, of your own accord, is the power of your free will, which is the master of the household of your being.

Besides, you are conscious in yourself of an intellectual and spiritual life that goes on in union with the life of your body, but superior to it. You reason, which brutes cannot do. You will and make decisions. You are a self-governing being. Animals, we know, act entirely from instinct and impulse, although they may seem to have something like intelligence. We use the word *intelligence* in their regard in a different sense from that in which we use it to describe the actions of men. Animals cannot advance in intellectual power. They cannot determine their own actions freely; they have no free will. But your free will is the rudder of your ship of life. It is the dominating power of your destiny. It can determine your present and your future.

The one being whose actions cannot ever be calculated entirely beforehand is the intellectual and free being — man. Of course, man is also greatly influenced by impulse and instincts. He is a creature of habit and is likely to do again what he has done before. He is apt to imitate others. All these things have an influence on his free will, but they do not absolutely control it. At any time, a person may rise against his habits and change them. He may suddenly decide to break with his former ways of conduct, and, without any reason except his own free will, he may quit the crowd and act in a way that is unsocial and different from others. In other words, he is always free to will other than what he has chosen to will before.

The will is the master of the household of your being because, either directly or indirectly, by its command or its control, it can make or unmake you, can change the current of your life, can tear down and build up your character. By choosing what is good, upright, and noble, you can constantly improve and ennoble your own being. By yielding, weakly and foolishly, to what is wrong and base, you can destroy and ruin your own character.

The will responds marvelously to exercise, and this singular faculty can control itself and improve itself, by taking firm resolutions and by insisting on different ways of action.

The growth of the will through exercise may be compared to that of the muscle of your arm. Every time you move that muscle, vigorously and definitely, it becomes just a trifle stronger. Even delicate measurements can hardly detect the result of only a few tensings and relaxings of the muscle. But if you persist, day after day, in doing regular exercise, you can readily see that the muscle becomes more and more developed, its strength increases, and, after a little while, you can handle weights that before you could not have lifted.

In a similar way, your will is constantly strengthened or weakened by your actions. Every time you will strongly, rightly, and vigorously, your will becomes stronger, more correct, and more vigorous. Every time you will to do what is wrong or ignoble, your will becomes to that extent inclined to what is ignoble and wrong. It is always a little easier to do what you have done before. If your will is accustomed to yield to persuasion, it acquires the habit of yielding. If it grows used to standing out against difficulties and persisting in its resolve, it acquires those habits also.

There is nothing to which you cannot aspire in the matter of training the will, if only you are patient and constant in your exercise of that faculty. Experience has shown that weak-willed persons can become strong and determined. Those whose will is encrusted with bad habits can shake off those habits and replace them by virtue. But this can never be done suddenly or easily. It would be no less foolish to expect to leap into the prize ring, full of vigor, strength, and resistance, without exercise and without training, than it would to hope to have a correct, strong, and vigorous will, without the discipline and effort of that faculty.

Chapter Twenty

Let reason guide you

We have been speaking about the cultivation of a strong will, a firm, decided character, but it will be useful in this connection to say a few words concerning that counterfeit of strength of will that we call stubbornness. It is as undesirable to be stubborn as it is desirable to be firm and strong-willed. Yet not a few confound the one with the other in their daily lives, and when they think themselves strong and firm, they are really only obstinate and stubborn.

When we speak of a stubborn person nowadays, we mean one who is difficult to handle or deal with, refractory, obstinate, unreasonably persistent in his own views and in his own determination. Such a person is a nuisance, a pest. He is a source of inconvenience to those around him, and his stubbornness and unreasonable inflexibility make him often a burden to himself as well as to other people.

What is the difference between stubbornness and firm character, between the stubborn will and the will that is disciplined and firm for good? The difference is to be found in the reasonableness of one's actions. A person with a strong will, disciplined and determined, will be firm and constant in his resolution so long as there is no reason for changing the determination he once has adopted. He is inflexible in resisting opposition and overcoming obstacles so long as his good sense tells him that to be firm and inflexible is a virtue. But if you can give him good reasons for changing his determination, reasons that are better than those which have persuaded him to adopt a certain course, then he will yield and change his resolution without insisting on having his own way merely because it is his own way.

The stubborn person, on the other hand, is unreasonable in his dogged determination to have his way. He wants his way because it is his way, not because it is better or more reasonable. He insists on doing as he likes because he likes it. For such a man, the reasons that others bring forward have little value. The preferences of others and their mature judgment do not influence him as they should. He will because he will, and he won't because he won't, and that is an end of it. Such a person cannot be swayed by reasonable argument. If he cannot be compelled to change his mind by actual force or be scared into it or made docile by some promise of gain, then he had better be let alone. There is no dealing with him.

Now, while we carefully cultivate our power of will, we should always keep it subject to reason. A reasonable strength of determination is always excellent. A dogged determination of will, unguided by reason, becomes stubbornness. We should, therefore, weigh the motives we have for firmly determining upon a certain line of action. We should be open-minded, so that, if anyone else has suggestions to make, we will gladly give them due consideration, and we should be courteously willing to yield when we are shown to be in the wrong.

This fine courtesy and noble capacity of changing our mind when we are wrong is entirely compatible with the strongest and firmest willpower. A highly cultivated will, guided by a calm, judicious, and cultured intelligence, gives us the ideal character, in no way stubborn, but absolutely firm. It is decided but not domineering, and capable of altering decisions when new facts require it. It is capable, too, of holding strongly to a line of action, so long as there is no really good reason for changing one's course.

The truly great heroes of humanity all offer us examples of noble firmness, a mighty power of will devoid of stubbornness. Consider Louis IX of France, that excellent knight, that king and gentleman without reproach. He was the soul of gentleness and courtesy, yet his will was firm as steel, as strong and supple as the bright blade he wore at his side. Consider Joan of Arc, that wonderful maiden, who, despite the weakness of her sex and the tenderness of her youth, led the beaten and discouraged armies of her people against the invader and broke his power in her native land. She was the soul of courage, determination, firmness, and yet was full of meekness, gentleness, and courtesy. Consider, again, our own national heroes Washington and Lincoln, who, in great crises of history, held firm with a moral power that was as flexible and adaptable as it was strong and steadfast in the face of danger. Men who were merely stubborn would have alienated their friends and supporters, would have rushed headlong into danger, would have insisted on their own way in spite of the judgment of others. But these men showed moral courage without stubbornness.

Glancing at the circle of your friends, you will see, perhaps, some lesser heroes, men and women who have never achieved and never will attain anything like public greatness, but who have strong, noble characters, firm, unyielding in the face of trials, and yet devoid of stubbornness. They can change their decisions to meet changing circumstances. They do not cleave to their own opinions and their own desires merely because of personal preferences. They are strong, and yet they are kind. Other men and women who will come within your personal observation are weak, but stubborn. When it comes to questions of great principle, they may be easily overcome, but they stick to some small point of personal preference as though life itself were involved in their having their own way.

By comparing these two extremes and pondering them, you will be able to see better what decisions you ought to make about your own personal character, how you should uproot in it all that makes for stubbornness and cultivate instead a reasonable, kindly, firm, but courteous willpower. Thus, you will be able to steer a middle course between weakness and stubbornness and will be able to cultivate the moral fiber of your will without becoming obstinate, perverse, and disagreeable.

Chapter Twenty-One

Choose worthwhile amusements

In the choice of amusements, people, especially the young, often show a singular lack of prudence. Nowadays, amusement is looked on as almost as necessary as food and drink. People will have entertainment, and perhaps they need it more now than in simpler times, because the strain of modern life is greater and therefore demands more systematic relaxation. But it makes a tremendous difference what sort of amusement one chooses.

Some amusements are elevating, others are merely indifferent, and still others are degrading. Some amusements tense the nerves and strain the attention; others relax the nerves and refresh the mind. Some amusements give valuable information and a cheerful, sane outlook on the world. Others tend to warp and distort our views on life and to give us false principles and ideas. Some amusements squander money, others are economical, and still others are free as the air.

Some amusements give helpful, physical exercise; others keep men and women in stuffy, ill-ventilated rooms where their health is injured rather than improved. Some amusements cultivate the intelligence and help the imagination. Some form the feelings and emotions; some again are merely ignorant and show a foolish or a childish mind. By reflecting for a few moments, you will probably be able to classify almost all the amusements that you know under one of these heads.

It will be well worth your while to reflect as to what amusements you chiefly patronize and why you prefer the ones you choose. Do you select your amusements according to your own judgment, or someone else's? Do you follow the crowd and merely entertain yourself as everyone does, or is there some individuality about your preferences? Does your taste run toward elevated amusements or toward cheap and common ones?

A man's true character is often more accurately indicated by his choice of amusements than by almost any other element in his conduct. In business and society, people are on their guard and conceal their preferences to a certain degree. But when they choose their amusements, they are likely to express their personality quite frankly. People who merely drift with the crowd and make no real choice of amusements at all, taking up now one thing, now another, as the crowd chooses, are likely to be people of very little individuality, of a very ordinary character. Those whose amusements tend to the intellectual and the refined are pretty sure to be people of intelligence and refinement.

Not only does your choice of amusement indicate your character, but it also influences it to a notable degree. When you amuse yourself, especially if it is an amusement such as attending a movie, a play, or an opera, or reading a book, you lay yourself open to deep impressions, because you are off your guard. The very nature of an amusement is that it seeks to please and entertain in itself.

When what we call "propaganda" comes into amusement, it is usually introduced with great care, so as not to be obvious, just as medicine may be hidden in a spoonful of jelly. Thus, people swallow poisonous principles more readily through amusements than in almost any other way. They are pleased and interested, they sympathize with the thoughts or the fancies of the writer or the composer, and, before they realize it, they find themselves agreeing with the principles that are adroitly insinuated through the amusement.

You ought to scrutinize your amusements very carefully for the sake both of your self-respect and your self-development. An endless variety of entertainment is offered nowadays; good music and good drama are ready to hand, and both are elevating and refining. Art is at your service in well-stocked galleries in every city of importance and in hundreds of beautifully illustrated books describing the work of the great masters. Realize the momentousness of seeking out these things and choosing them for your amusement. You live in an age rich beyond comparison in opportunities.

The world of books is also a lovely and congenial world, in which, if your taste is cultured and your instincts true, you will never weary of wandering. We are richer than in previous ages, because we inherit all the culture of former ages in the most accessible forms, in libraries, in museums, and in schools and universities. The poorest person of today has far more opportunities for reading than had the wealthiest person of former times.

Of all amusements, a walk in the country with a congenial friend is one of the most delightful, whether in spring, when the world is awakening, or in summer, when the evidence of

God's great creative power lies all around, or in autumn, when the forests are gleaming with crimson and gold, or in vigorous winter, when, beneath the snow and ice, the woodlands sleep, full of life, waiting expectantly the dawn of the spring.

So take to heart this honest suggestion that you evaluate your own amusements and try to improve your choice of them. Your capacity for happiness and pleasure will not be lessened, but will grow with the elevation of your taste and with the cultivation of prudence in your choice of entertainments.

Chapter Twenty-Two

Take care of your body

You should wish to have a strong and healthy body, not out of personal vanity, or so that you may "feel good" every day, but principally because your body is the dwelling of your spirit, and you can never do your full duty to yourself and to others unless you take a reasonable care of your health.

There are two extremes in this matter. One is to neglect one's physical well-being, and the other is to think too much of it, and both are harmful.

If you think too much of your health, you will become morbid, or else you will sacrifice higher interests for the sake of keeping fit. Bodily health is only a means to an end, and not an end in itself, and sometimes a person even has to disregard his health to perform some duty or to achieve some higher good.

Besides, thinking too much of their health actually makes people ill. They become sick with imaginary diseases. If you think of your little finger for a long time, it will begin to be uncomfortable, just because of the attention you focus on it. So, when people are worrying about their heart, or about their lungs, or about their digestion, they tend to grow ill from too much attention to health.

The general principles of health are quite plain. Get enough exercise in the open air, but not too much. Eat enough substantial and healthful food, but, again, not too much. Get enough sleep, plenty of fresh air, an abundance of pure water, as much sunshine as you need, and reasonable and helpful recreation. Finally, maintain a calm and happy spirit. These are the essentials for good health.

The right sort of recreation also has a good deal to do with health, especially with the health of the nerves. The nervous system snaps when it is kept at too taut a tension and is made to work too constantly. The right sort of recreation gives relaxation to the nervous system, distracts the attention from our usual cares and responsibilities, and stores up in us new energy for the serious business of life. But recreation has to be chosen carefully to this end. A good many modern amusements are really more of a strain on the nervous system than a relaxation, and they tend to injure health rather than help it.

One's mental attitude has a great deal more to do with his health than many people realize. A cheerful, kindly, alert, interested temperament tends to good health, whereas worry, melancholy, dolefulness, overstrain, and selfish introspection are as unhealthy for the body as they are for the soul.

A faithful religious life, full of faith, hope and charity toward God and man, has a wonderful influence on the health of the body as well as of the spirit. The interaction of the body and the soul is not sufficiently realized, even today, although more and more stress is being put on it from the medical side. Many so-called faith cures have their origin, not in any extraordinary powers, but in the ordinary reaction of the mind on the body.

You should also remember that what a person does to his body in the way either of care or abuse during his young years will be visited on him in his old age. Because young people have a surplus of life and energy, they often neglect the laws of health and go to excesses either in work or amusement. The reaction does not make itself felt at once, but in later years, they bitterly regret that they have drained the strength of their constitution by the early disregard of the principles of health.

All in all, this is an extremely important subject from the standpoint of true success in life. A sickly, weak person who has to struggle against constitutional infirmities is always at a disadvantage. He cannot put forth his whole energy. It is true that strength of will and firm purpose can often wonderfully overcome the weakness of the body. Still, why should a young person deliberately and foolishly handicap himself by neglecting his health in early years, instead of giving his more mature age the advantage of physical powers that have been strengthened by exercise and preserved by a normal life?

If you happen to be of a weak constitution, do not be discouraged by your sickness, because it gives you an opportunity for still more heroic achievement by triumphing over its handicap. But if you are strong, preserve your health and strength by reasonable care. You will need every help you can get in the strenuous and tiring race toward worthy achievement.

Chapter Twenty-Three

Maintain a healthy mind

A healthy mind is even more precious than a healthy body. It is far better to have a healthy mind and a diseased body than a diseased mind even in a body that is bursting with health. A healthy mind can disregard pain and sickness, can endure sorrow, and can be happy even in the midst of wretchedness.

Now, as there are rules of health for keeping the body fit, so there are rules for keeping the mind fit. Many elements that enter into the life of the body, enter, in a different form, into the life of the mind. We have remarked how important good food is for bodily health. It must be pure, nourishing, well proportioned, and in just a sufficient quantity. In the same way, the mind must have "food" that is pure, proportionate, and sufficient.

Our mental food comes to us in various ways. The things we see stir up thoughts within us. So do the things we hear from others; so also do the things we read. All these can be food for the mind, or they may be poison. They are what the mind takes in and digests, in its own way. They are the material that prompts our thoughts. The mind feeds itself, in a sense, by dwelling on certain topics, by choosing to reflect on certain themes.

Now, the food of our mind must always be pure. No good can come out of evil thoughts. You do yourself an intolerable wrong if you allow your mind to dwell upon and digest anything that is evil. The writers of immoral books, propounders of evil theories, are really public malefactors. Some of them are worse than murderers, because they kill not bodies but souls, the most precious part of men. What an extreme of folly it is deliberately to gulp down the mental poisons of immoral books!

You ought to take the same precaution in regard to the conversation you listen to, the things you observe, and all the material for thought that you give your mind. Insist that it be elevated and pure. Never allow your mind to dwell on anything that is not right and good.

You ought to proportion, too, the food of your mind, so that your thoughts may be truly nourished. To read wholesome lightweight literature may do you good. To read nothing but lightweight literature is to nourish your mind on froth. Make your interests somewhat broad and human. Do not cleave to only one group of thoughts or interests. Widen your intelligent appreciation of literature, art, and science. Give your mind a well-balanced ration of various nourishing foods.

Besides food, your mind also requires exercise for its good health. Dull, stagnant minds often become diseased. Minds that dwell too much on a single thought are likely to become morbid. Have various interests. Acquire the faculty of being able to take other people's viewpoints and to sympathize with them. Learning another language and reading different literature are charming exercises for the mind. Many who have succeeded greatly in professional posts have made it a practice of exercising their minds in some study quite different from the one that is their lifework.

The mind sometimes needs a rest, but it rests chiefly by a change of occupation. When you sleep, your mind reposes too, but sometimes your imagination keeps busy, in dreaming. During all your waking hours, that restless intelligence of yours is constantly reasoning, remembering, reflecting, forming judgments, and suggesting decisions to your will.

Good lightweight literature, entertaining conversations, and worthwhile amusements all rest the mind. Those who know how to vary their intellectual labor with the right sort of recreation are the ones who last longest as thinkers and do the best work.

The give-and-take of interesting conversation is excellent exercise for the mind. You cannot always choose the subject of conversation, but you can tactfully influence the choice, and you can interest your friends in following lines of thought that will be helpful and useful. Mere trivial conversation, especially the loose banter and cheap slang that one hears so much today, makes for mental dissipation, not exercise.

Whom you talk to and what you talk about make a very great difference to your mental development and strength. Those who listen to unworthy talk and stories, who read what is evil, deliberately debase themselves and grow in evil knowledge day by day. Those who are wise enough to keep close watch on their thoughts, to have a deep respect for their own minds, and to maintain the interest and integrity of their thought grow in nobleness day by day.

Chapter Twenty-Four

Think kindly of others

Two persons are brought into contact with a third person. One looks at once for all the good points in that person's character, appreciates them very much, and emulates them. The defects perceived will appear to this kind person only as shadows, which set off in relief the person's good qualities. The second person will begin to notice immediately the defects and faults in that character. He will grow vexed and irritated by them, will make them an occasion of suspecting still greater, but more hidden, shortcomings, and will hardly notice at all the fine qualities and noble traits that appeared to the first person as so much more worthy of notice and imitation.

These are two extremes of temperament: the very kind and the very critical. In between, one finds a whole series of mental attitudes. Some persons are prone to notice certain kinds of faults and to overlook others. Some especially appreciate certain types of good qualities and minimize other types that may be actually more precious. If you analyze your own attitude and your own customary way of judging others, you will probably find something here to regret and correct.

Which of the above two points of view is more correct, more praiseworthy and estimable? Which makes the possessor more happy? Without doubt, it is the kind person who is more fortunate, because he lives in a world full of sunshine. He sees the best in everyone around him. He is cheered by the sight of other people's good qualities and stirred thereby to be better himself.

The unkind person lives in a gloomy atmosphere, vexed by other people's too obvious shortcomings. He discounts all the sunshine about him and emphasizes the gloom. He is sour and ill-natured, because he dwells on unpleasant characteristics.

The two attitudes of mind are neatly characterized in the following lines: "Two men looked out from their prison bars; one saw mud, and the other saw stars." There is always a good deal of mud to be seen if one wishes to look for it, but looking at mud is a depressing and gloomy occupation. There are usually a good many stars to be seen, if one has an eye for stars; and looking at stars is cheering, calming, and elevating to the soul.

It is unfortunately true that many human beings naturally have a very keen eye for their own good qualities and a blind eye for their own defects, while they usually have a very sharp glance for their neighbor's defects and a duller vision for his good qualities. The individual who is by nature very prone to think kindly of others and to look on their better side is singularly blessed. But everyone can cultivate that attitude of kind judgment by deliberate practice.

Set yourself to find out and to esteem the better qualities in those around you, and you will be surprised at how many good qualities they possess. Even persons whom you may perhaps consider quite wicked may have noble traits and characteristics in them that far outshine your corresponding qualities.

Their wickedness may be only apparent; they may have a twisted conscience, false ideas of right and wrong, or they may be the victims of circumstances or under the influence of bad habits, which have been occasioned by some physical fault or weakness. But the good that is within them is probably very genuine; at least, you ought to consider it so, as you yourself are eager to have everyone estimate your good qualities at their highest value and to discount your imperfections.

The goodness that we see in those around us should seem doubly precious to us, because men and women are under such severe strains and temptations that even a little virtue in them is quite honorable. This is the way you will do well to judge others. Consider that it is much to their credit to possess the good qualities they show. But if you could penetrate beneath the surface and see how many struggles and victories are to their credit, how many temptations they feel, but do not yield to, and how often they will to do good deeds and to show generosity and forgiveness, then your esteem for them would grow. You may well think that if you were placed in the position of many of those around you, with their training or lack of it, their inward difficulties and outward allurements, you would not be as good as they.

By thus thinking kindly of all, you also do yourself a great service. If you seek out and recognize the finest and best traits of human nature, you yourself become finer and better. Besides, you come far nearer to the actual truth than does the uncharitable or unkind man, because, as a matter of fact, people are really better than they seem, and it is the finer, worthier side of human nature that is the truer and more real. Faults are much more obtrusive than are virtues. But goodness is deliberate and intended, while wickedness often springs from weakness and inadvertence.

In thus acting, you will surely be treating others as you would like them to treat you. Those who have a kind viewpoint are well-loved, respected, and honored for their kindness. Critical, censorious, evil-thinking people are instinctively shunned by others, because no one wishes his virtues to be minimized and his faults exaggerated.

Surely these are strong motives for cultivating a kind viewpoint toward the whole world. And beware of being limited in your kindness. Let the sunshine of your appreciation and genuine esteem pour forth on all people, and, in turn, people will be drawn to you.

Chapter Twenty-Five

Resist temptations

It has been very well said that the difference between an upright person and a rascal is not that one has temptations and the other none, but that one has temptations and struggles with them, and the other has temptations and yields. Sometimes it is the one who has the greater temptations who leads the better life, because he has a strong will and an upright resolve that keep him battling against temptations. Thus he gains strength of character and firmness of purpose from the very necessity he has of continual resistance to bad impulses. To have temptations and resist them is a very effective form of moral exercise, while to be without temptations very often means to be without occasions of self-conquest.

We should therefore look upon every temptation as a summons to battle and an opportunity for victory. Never get discouraged or downhearted at the frequency or violence of your impulses to evil, so long as you have the will to resist and the strength to overcome them. It is common to human nature to have temptations. People differ only in the nature of their temptations and the strength of their resistance.

The temptations against which a person has to struggle are to some degree an indication of his character. Weak natures are tempted to yield to others, to follow bad example, to compromise with principle, and to neglect duty. Strong natures are tempted to domineer, to exert their strength unjustly, and to tyrannize over others. Some people are strongly tempted to pride, but scorn the pleasures of the body. Others are tempted to excesses in eating and drinking, but have no difficulty in the matter of pride.

If you get to know yourself and analyze your own character correctly, you will find that most of your temptations center on some predominant fault, some leading tendency to evil in you, and if you guard yourself against that fault and cultivate the contrary virtue, you will be largely protected against yielding to temptations. It may be that this fault is mere sloth and weakness of character, and if you build up habits of industry, you can overcome the temptations that arise from laziness. It may be that most of your temptations arise from excessive self-esteem, and, by cultivating the habits of modesty and consideration for others, you can discipline this chief fault of yours. Perhaps your principal fault is excessive selfishness, and your temptations will then be overcome by developing a habit of being generous to others.

It requires definite resolve and strong will to overcome these tendencies, but once you have a firm grip on your own weaknesses, you will be much happier and more contented. This peace of mind and calmness of conscience is worth far more than the dubious pleasure you might have had in yielding to your weaknesses.

Temptations are merely an invitation to purchase a little passing pleasure at the cost of forfeiting lasting happiness. We have already seen that pleasure and happiness are two entirely different things — that happiness brings content and peace, whereas pleasure merely gives a passing gratification of some faculty.

Now, what temptations offer us is almost always a passing gratification and the fact that this gratification is to be bought by some yielding of principle, some action against conscience, means that when the temporary gratification is gone, the stings of conscience and the degradation of character will remain. For instance, suppose a person is tempted to commit an act of injustice against another in order to get some money. The apparent good that makes him wish to commit this act of injustice is the money he will get. He is quite aware that to cheat another person is a mean and contemptible action, and his conscience urges him not to do it. But the temporary gratification of getting the money proves too strong for his weak will, and he commits the act of injustice and takes the money. What has he got by yielding to the temptation? He has, on the one hand, remorse of conscience, a loss of his self-esteem, and future retribution and, on the other, the possession of money that does not belong to him.

We can easily see the foolishness of such an action. Its perpetrator will either spend the money, lose it, give it away, or keep it and die with it in his possession, and in any one of these cases, the money may give him only a passing gratification. But he will keep permanently the guilt, the shame, and the self-contempt that come from the performance of a mean, unworthy action. If he had been brave enough and strong enough to resist the temptation, he would have sacrificed the passing gratification of possessing money that did not belong to him, but he would have kept the content and happiness of having overcome a base impulse and having acted according to his better nature.

Besides, every temptation yielded to means a distinct weakening of moral fiber and a tendency to do the same unworthy action when the occasion arises; whereas every resolute conquest of a temptation leaves a person so much the stronger on the next occasion, and so much the more able to act nobly when he is tempted again. One who is tempted to drunkenness feels the inclination to accept the passing pleasure and gratification of conviviality, stimulation, and forgetfulness at the expense of his conscience and his self-respect. If he yields, he soon loses the passing pleasure of excessive drinking, but he keeps the guilt, the self-contempt, and the strengthening of his bad habit of excessive drinking.

A good many of your temptations, of course, come from within you, because every human faculty keeps craving satisfaction. But some of the worst temptations you will have to oppose will come from your friends and your associates. People like to make others become like themselves. An upright person tries to influence everyone to be upright, and a depraved character tends to try to make everyone depraved. Those who are given to some vice, such as drunkenness, are inclined to try to build up public opinion that is favorable to drunkenness, to get as many as possible of their friends to drink to excess. The same is true of other vices.

So, if you keep company with those who are dissolute in any respect, they will strongly influence you to become like them. Fellowship and public opinion are hard things to go against, and if you wish to avoid yielding to temptation, you have to choose good friends accordingly.

This problem of temptations and their avoidance and conquest runs through the whole of life. Wherever you go, you carry your own self, and hence you will be continuously at war with your own weaknesses. Yet it is not in being free from temptations that a person's nobility consists, but in overcoming them bravely. In that way lies peace and real, lasting happiness. So although you will never be without struggle as long as you live, you will always have opportunities for gaining victories.

Chapter Twenty-Six

Gain mastery over yourself

It has often been said, and truly, that the greatest victory a man can gain is the victory over himself. Caesar conquered the world, but he did not conquer himself. Alexander subdued nations, but failed to achieve self-conquest. Napoleon was able to dominate almost all around him, but not himself. The great conquerors have been laid low by their own passions, their own ambitions, and their own human weaknesses. Their wills were powerful enough to subdue millions of others, but not strong enough to subdue themselves.

One reason for the difficulty of self-conquest is that we must inflict pain and sorrow on ourselves to achieve it. You may have, in your character and disposition, certain elements that are out of equilibrium. It may be that you are subject to an unreasonable craving for possessions, and unless you dominate it, it will destroy you. It may be that the pleasures of the body attract you to an excessive degree; if you do not curb them, they will ruin you, body and soul. It may be that you are a victim of laziness and sloth, and unless you shake off that torpid spirit, it will make of you a shirker and a laggard. Perhaps anger and envy grow like an evil ferment in your character, and unless you moderate and control them, they will sour your whole nature.

Whatever your predominant fault or prevailing passion may be, find it out. Put a bridle on it. Drive it hard with acts of self-discipline and self-denial, until you feel that it is under control and that you have it on a tight rein. You will then find it pulling and struggling still, perhaps, but it will be carrying you forward where you want to go, instead of dragging you, like a runaway steed, helplessly onward to disaster.

There is no escaping this struggle with ourselves if we wish to be master. Let a horse run wild in the fields and never suffer the touch of the bit or the pain of the whip, and it will be a useless animal, or if you do drive it to a wagon, it will kick over the traces and wreck your vehicle. But put that same horse in training, teach it to go this way and that at the touch of the rein, and to speed forward in a straight line at the crack of the whip, and you have a serviceable and docile beast to carry you wherever you will.

It is so with a passion. Let it run wild, and it will be the master. It will drag you wherever it will, and you will have little control over its vagaries. But train it, and keep it under discipline, and it will be a source of strength and help to you.

The means of self-conquest are to be found in daily acts of self-discipline and self-denial. The impulse that is strongest in you is especially to be curbed systematically by little acts of mortification. If you are prone to anger and envy, make weariless acts, in word, look, and deed, of gentleness and generosity. If you have an excessive craving for indulgence in food and drink, or for the other pleasures of the body, make your body often feel the sting of denial, deliberately curbing it just when it most wishes satiety. If you are slothful, make your will lash your faculties into action with more alertness. Spring out of bed a few moments before the time appointed. Arrive at your work a little before the moment when you must be there, and then insist on keeping up a steady effort when you most feel like stopping and idling.

Every day offers you renewed opportunities for this practical self-discipline. Your master instinct, your leading passion, is continually stirred up by the events of every day. You find yourself now inclined to one excess and now tempted to another, and your conscience is always urging you to resist those impulses. But this resistance needs a definite, strenuous effort of your will. Act according to conscience, and whip down the swelling of passion. Are you prone to anger? A dozen times a day someone will vex you, and even though you may not show any outward signs, you may curse in your heart, if you yield to anger. Each of those dozen vexations is one more opportunity of self-conquest, and if you curb yourself, time after time, you will find growing within you the habit of self-mastery, the glorious power to preserve your inward equanimity of soul, no matter what those around you may do or say to you.

If you are inclined to be slothful, you will find a score of opportunities during the day of wasting time, of shirking your work, of resting when you should be active. Every one of these opportunities of sloth is a definite chance to exercise self-mastery, by doing the very opposite of what you feel inclined to do, by working when you are tempted to be idle.

If you are proud, your pride will be rubbed often during the day by slight hurts and negligences, or perhaps by open insults, and many times you will be inclined to speak a boastful word or to act from ostentation. When these impulses come, down them vigorously, refuse to be disturbed by outward insults and refuse as well to speak boastful words or to be mastered by the impulse to show off.

If you do these things each day, you will acquire stronger and stronger self-control. You will become the captain of your own soul, the master of your own destiny. The beach that hems in the ocean and stops its tempestuous waves is made up of an endless number of grains of sand; each is in itself an insignificant thing, but taken together they present an impassable barrier to the waves. So it is with the habits of self-control you form. They are made up of an endless number of small actions of self-discipline, each slight and insignificant, but which, taken altogether, form a bulwark against the strongest tempests of passion.

It is a fine ambition to desire to be master of yourself, to have your passions well in check and to be able to live a pure, kind, earnest, and serviceable life in spite of all allurements and obstacles, in spite of all the stormy waves of passion. But there is only one way to achieve this ambition. You will never gain self-mastery by merely desiring it, or by dreaming of it, or by considering in theory its nature and efficacy. The only means of truly achieving this priceless victory is by constant, daily courage and perseverance in waging small battles with yourself and gaining small, but most momentous, victories.

Chapter Twenty-Seven

Distinguish between true good and false good

In everything you do, you seek some good. But there are true goods and false goods, things that are really worthwhile working for and suffering for and other things that only appear to be desirable, but are really not so. The true successes of life come from encouraging the solidly good things and going against those that are vain and foolish. The only safe guide in deciding whether a thing is good and worthwhile or merely has a false appearance of good is your reason, enlightened by faith. If you act reasonably and seek reasonable, good things, you will always be happy.

Let us illustrate with an example. A young man is just starting to practice law. He is full of energy, enthusiasm, and earnestness. At the same time, his appetite for amusement and pleasure is still very strong. He is brought face-to-face with the unavoidable fact that there is not enough time in a day to do all he would like to do. He has to choose, therefore, between various goods that offer themselves for the price of time. He sincerely wishes to succeed in his profession. At the same time, he would like to have a good time. He is distracted between conflicting urges. Now, he feels that he ought to devote all his energies to law, to acquiring a practice, and to building up a reputation for industry. This is a solid good. His reason tells him that what is worth doing is worth doing well and that he ought to work hard at his profession. At the same time, social life is very attractive to him. Exciting amusements, late hours, and even dissipation appeal to him strongly, but they offer only an apparent good, and his reason tells him that these things are not worthwhile, that they merely bring a temporary satisfaction, but that he would do much better to avoid them for the sake of his practice.

Now, if this young man follows the guidance of reason, he will be safe. He will calmly put aside the allurements of pleasure, dissipation, and even of innocent and harmless activities that would distract him from his work. In this way, he will grow stronger, through self-conquest, and wiser, by following his reason. As time goes on, his honestly earned success in his profession, his personal integrity, and the esteem of his fellowmen will make him happy, because he has chosen the genuinely good things and rejected the apparently good ones.

But this same young man might have freely chosen to neglect his duty, or at least to disregard it a little, to take time from his work for pleasure, staying up late at night so as not to be fit for work the next morning, and so on. In other words, he might have sold the solid success to be attained through care, diligence, and steady work in exchange for passing and flimsy gratifications. The decision rests with him, but he must abide by the consequences. He can take the pleasure if he wishes it, but then he must do without success. He can choose the apparent good if he prefers and can act against his reason, but then he may not complain about the retribution that follows.

You are constantly occupied in making very similar choices. Every day brings its array of truly good things and apparently good things, which offer themselves to you all along the path of your life. Unfortunately, the apparently good things, which are really deceptive and worthless, seem often more attractive than the solid benefits of life. There are various reasons for this, one of which is that we are creatures of feelings and passions, and our reason does not maintain its rule over our lives. If we were born with only reason and will, it would be much easier to act discreetly; but as soon as a bodily gratification is offered to us, our bodily impulses grow extremely eager to possess it.

Thus, if you offer to a famished man some appetizing food, he has an almost irresistible impulse to devour it, even though he knows it is dangerous for him to do so. So, also, a man who is given to strong drink, but who knows how perilous it is for him to indulge, will nevertheless drink himself silly because of the craving he feels for alcoholic stimulant.

Hence, we must perpetually resist wayward feelings and impulses, and perpetually insist on following reason and on rejecting the apparently good things that will make us neglect solid and worthwhile good.

Chapter Twenty-Eight

Do not fear what others think

We all have a natural fear of displeasing others, of doing anything that will call down on us their criticism and disapproval. In its place, this instinct is helpful; it can be used to strengthen our determination to succeed in life and to lead an upright life.

But excessive fear of what other people think is a dreadful danger to a person and ruins many a career. Public opinion is not always right; in fact, it is sure to be wrong frequently. Great people usually have to go through a period of definite struggle and warfare against public opinion until they grow strong enough to shape public opinion themselves. After that, public opinion may help them more than it hinders them.

Everyone who realizes the possibilities in him and makes a solid success in life must, to his own degree, go against public opinion. Sometimes it speaks to him out of his own family circle. "Why do you want to put yourself forward? What's the use of making yourself a slave to your work? Go out and have a good time like other people! You do not want to make yourself a plaster saint, or to grow old before your time." When his own friends and family say these things to someone, he has to stiffen himself to a twofold resistance and have a double share of determination to go on. He realizes then how true it is that a man's enemies are of his own household.[9]

But whether you get encouragement in your own family or not, you certainly will meet with discouragement from the broad circle of your acquaintances. There is a native jealousy in mankind that makes many people resent anyone's pushing himself forward and upward. Everyone likes everyone else to be as he is. Hence, if you begin to work especially hard and to go forward with particular courage, you will have to face a certain amount of disapproval. If you let it discourage you and pull you down, then you have weakly surrendered to public opinion.

In the same way, the influence of those around you often tries to make you do what everybody else does and be what everybody is. In a group of young people, if one frowns on bad talk or refuses to engage in dubious amusements, he immediately becomes sensible of the terrific pull of public opinion. "Why aren't you like the rest of the crowd? Why do you put yourself before everybody else? What is good enough for us is good enough for you." This is the spoken or unspoken attitude and sentiment of the rest of the group.

Now, it takes all of one's prudence, justice, temperance, and especially fortitude to go against public opinion when it is evil and to use it only when it is good. We all, by nature, desire the approval of those around us. This is a very good thing up to a certain point, because it offers us an incentive for effort, a reason for trying to succeed in life. In some things, the judgments of public opinion are correct. It insists on friendliness

[9] Cf. Matt. 10:36.

and comradeship. It wishes people to be sociable and kind. It encourages generosity and good will.

Hence, as far as it helps us on in the right direction, we ought to use it. But the time to begin to resist public opinion is precisely where it departs from right reason. You ought to get in the habit of bringing everything under the examination of honest reason and of following the dictates of your intellect and not of your feelings and imagination. Where we perceive that the opinion of those around us in our regard is wrong, that it is pulling us back and holding us down, we ought to begin a brave battle against it.

It requires prudence to see just where the starting point of that battle ought to be, where concern for what others think ceases to be reasonable and becomes a hindrance to us. We need justice, too, to deal properly with what others think, because we owe others a certain amount of consideration. We have duties toward them, just as they have to us. Hence, our prudence and justice will incline us to deal kindly and gently with others and to antagonize them as little as possible, while at the same time we do what we think right in spite of others' opinion.

Very often one courageous person, by his way of acting, will rouse a storm of public disapproval on account of his lack of tact and prudence, while another person, going just as directly against public opinion for a good cause, will do it tactfully and gently and will avoid almost entirely, or at least to a great degree, the storm of protest that the other stirs up through his tactlessness or inconsiderateness.

We need temperance in resisting public opinion, for everything ought to be done gently, moderately, and in due order.

We should not anger others unnecessarily and should disturb them as little as possible. Of course, there are some occasions when it is necessary frankly and definitely to fly in the face of public opinion. However, a modest and temperate attitude, without self-assertiveness or egotism, will usually be successful in averting angry feelings when intemperate zeal or self-assertiveness irritate others needlessly.

We need fortitude, to a great degree, to carry us through the difficulties and discouragements that fear of others' opinion will stir up against us when we are attempting anything noteworthy and out of the usual. It takes special courage of a very fine and high kind to disregard the disapproval of others, and the nearer and dearer they are to us, the more courage is required. Men who can look without flinching into a cannon's mouth very often weakly surrender or run away before the frown of public opinion.

Call yourself before the bar of your own judgment, and examine just how you deal with public opinion. Do you exercise prudence in disregarding it in your regard? Are you just toward others in antagonizing them as little as possible? Is your attitude temperate and moderate and tactful, and at the same time, do you have the courage and firmness to go right ahead with what you see is just and reasonable, in spite of what people think? If you conquer this obstacle, you will have gone far toward making your life successful.

Chapter Twenty-Nine

Use criticism prudently

Criticism is a bitter but very potent medicine, particularly for the young. We can learn more about ourselves by looking through the eyes of others than through our own. It is pleasant to be praised and hard to be criticized, but of the two, criticism is sometimes endlessly better for us, if we can bear it well and use it rightly. Like every good remedy, criticism must be good and genuine, and it must be taken discreetly. You receive comments about you of various sorts, some favorable, some unfavorable, and both are useful. Bring favorable and unfavorable comments to the test of reason, and try to decide for yourself whether, and in how far, they are just.

Even as you are swayed by feelings, prejudice, and sentiment in what you say of others, so are they likely to be influenced in the same way in what they say of you. You have to discount their personal antipathies or affections to get at the true worth of their criticism. There are different sorts of criticism. Some will come to you spontaneously from those around you. This is the criticism of which you are continually sensible if you observe the actions and words of others in your regard.

For other criticism, you will have to ask discreet and wise friends, and you will be fortunate if they really tell you what they think of you. Your friends are usually much more inclined to tell the good they judge of you than to tell you their unfavorable opinions, while your enemies are unhappily inclined in the opposite direction and will more readily tell you the evil than the good. Hence it is a wise person who tries to get prudent criticism from his friends and to win praise from his enemies.

Generally speaking, others judge us better than we judge ourselves. They are more impartial and objective. We are too near to ourselves to see ourselves clearly without a great effort, and we are too well disposed to ourselves to judge ourselves severely enough. Much of the unconscious humor of life comes from the fact that people are so accurate in their estimate of others and so lenient and wrong in their opinion of themselves. You must know men and women who are as indignant at a fault in other people as they are addicted to the same fault themselves.

Hence, even those who do not have very good judgment in their own case may sometimes be very useful to you in pointing out your faults and helping you to correct them, but you must be able to weigh their criticism accurately in the scales of right reason and see whether it can help you, because it is just, or whether you ought to disregard it, because it is excessive.

The criticism of others may come to us both in words and in actions. We have remarked before that anger is a great truth-teller, and when people are very provoked with you, they are very apt to blurt out just what they think of you, which they had politely kept concealed until anger let down the bars of their discretion. When anyone utters an angry criticism against you, it is foolish to get angry in return, but you ought to ask yourself, "Just how true is that remark?" If it is true, you ought to profit by it. If it is false, disregard it.

We may as well start out with the conviction that we have a good many faults and defects, many of which we can correct quite effectively if we can only discover them in time. The question with you is not, "Do I have any faults to be corrected?" but rather, "Just what are my faults, and how should I correct them?" Left to yourself, you would have a very hard time realizing your own defects. The illumination given by others' criticism ought to be a great help in pointing out where you ought to get to work on your character.

Besides the spontaneous criticism that you will continually receive, you ought to seek criticism and advice, but only from wise people. Not everybody is fit to give you counsel. If you can find a really prudent person who wishes you well and yet can judge of you objectively, such an adviser will be a treasure for you. Yet even when you get such advice, you ought to turn it over in your mind, weigh it carefully, and see the reasonableness of it before you act.

Reason is the lighthouse of success in life, and no one else's reason can quite supply for your own. Advice will be of great help to you in assisting your own reason to see what is best for you, but you never ought to lean so much on another person's judgment as to surrender your own judgment weakly.

Most of all, you should never be discouraged by adverse criticism or very much surprised at it. The French moralist François de la Rochefoucauld, that very cynical student of human nature, remarks in one of his barbed paragraphs that no matter what good thing anyone says of us, we seldom are surprised at it. It is quite evident that we all like to have a good opinion of ourselves, but we ought to school ourselves to the opposite attitude of mind, so that no criticism we receive may much surprise or discourage us, but that all may set us thinking to find out and correct the latent faults in our conduct and character. To be discouraged because of criticism is very foolish. Either the criticism is false, and then we ought to disregard it — for why should a false criticism discourage us? — or it is true, or partly true, and then it ought to stir us to action, for all of our faults can be corrected, at least to some degree.

In the jostle and bustle of life, you will continually be rubbing against others and striking from them sparks of criticism, sometimes angry, sometimes vexed, but always valuable. Their actions will often speak more convincingly than their words. If you find people avoiding you, ask yourself why, and if you can find out the reason, it may throw great light on your character. Be slow to blame other people for not having a good opinion of you. It is much more profitable to blame yourself and usually truer, for other people are attracted to you or repelled by you instinctively because of what you are.

The general average of a man's esteem from others corresponds pretty closely to his character. Of course, this does not mean that the good are always appreciated or the evil always found out, but it does mean that in ordinary, average cases where a person is greatly esteemed and liked, it is often because of his personality, and where he is greatly disliked, it is often due to some fault in him.

It is very unprofitable for you to get the idea that other people are unreasonable in their treatment of you, and it is very profitable to take the attitude — without discouragement, however — that you ought to look first to see whether there are any defects in your own character before you blame others for not being kind to you.

This subject is extremely practical and immensely important in helping your success in life. Your use of criticism will go far either to make you or to break you. Make use of this strong, if bitter, medicine, which will tone your will, purify your resolutions, and show you just where and how to set about perfecting your character.

Chapter Thirty

Rely on your will, not on your feelings

You should draw a very clear distinction between the feelings and the will in your own mind and observe it in your conduct. For want of this distinction, many persons grieve unreasonably and suffer foolish regrets. Because they cannot control their feelings, they have a false sense of guilt, even when their will is right. Because they make too much of their feelings, they allow themselves to be carried away by them, when a strong will would keep them steadfast to duty.

The will is the master power within us of choosing between good and evil, of doing freely one of two alternatives, of acting or refusing to act, no matter what force or influence is brought to bear on us. The will is the one free faculty within us. It can determine itself and decide for itself between conflicting courses of action. When, after reflecting and weighing both sides of a question, we determine to follow one course of action and refuse another, this is an act of our free will.

It is only free actions for which we are accountable or can justly be praised or blamed. Actions that are spontaneous in us and beyond our control are not blameworthy, nor do they merit reward. We should not reproach ourselves for what we cannot help, but only for what we do freely and what we know, or should know, at the time, is evil. We should not give ourselves credit for what is not free either, but only for things over which we have control. Since it is our will that determines all free actions, it is only what is prompted by our will that gains for us merit or blame.

The feelings, on the other hand, are those inward sensations or emotions that come and go without our being able entirely to control them. At times, without knowing why, we feel depressed. At other times, for no particular reason, we become joyful and happy. When we meet one person for the first time, we feel an unaccountable attraction to him and become friends almost before we are well acquainted. We meet another person, and we feel an unaccountable repulsion and dislike, for which we have no reason at all and which we cannot explain except by saying that we feel averse to him. At times, we have feelings that are undevout and averse to good works. The next day our feelings may change, and we may be inclined to be very good and dutiful.

Now, all these impulses in us belong to the bodily part of our nature. Like the imagination, of which we have spoken before, they are dependent on bodily conditions. Hence, we are not always responsible for them. They do not affect our goodness except insofar as we willingly and freely yield to them. A person may have an extremely harsh and unfriendly disposition and, yet, by exercise of the will, may treat everyone with kindness and consideration. He deserves more credit than one whose feelings are all sociable and friendly. So, too, another may feel angry, harsh, and disagreeable, but, by an effort of his will, he may so control his feelings that he is courteous and obliging. All the more virtuous is he.

An upright and praiseworthy life is impossible without strict discipline of the feelings. The person who becomes a victim of his feelings and allows them to sway him this way and that is a pitiful object. He is like a ship without a rudder, driven before the wind. He is like someone mounted on a runaway horse, without bridle or spurs, not knowing where he is being borne or toward what catastrophe he is speeding on.

If you discipline your feelings and bring them under the control of good reason and will, they are splendid servants. One whose feelings are well ordered has a source of great power over others. An unfeeling, hard, and senseless person lacks the kind, human touch that influences those about him.

The feelings, like all other mighty forces, are, as the saying goes, good servants and tyrannous masters. Very strong feelings, well disciplined and well controlled, give a person moral strength and the power to travel far against adverse circumstances. They are like the fire beneath the boiler of an engine, like the steam that drives a train forward with dizzying speed. But those same feelings, allowed to master the spirit, are like steam in an explosion, rending and tearing, or like a fire fanned to a conflagration, burning and searing all with which it comes in touch.

The failure to control and discipline the feelings is often the source of great discouragement to young people. They confuse emotion with will, and temptation with consent; they think that merely because they have strong natural feelings, they are evil. This is by no means the case. Those with the strongest feelings sometimes gain the most merit, because they repress them bravely. It is not the experiencing of temptation that is wrong. It is the yielding to it. Temptations, however violent, and feelings, however masterful, are only occasions of merit, if they are disciplined and held in check by the free and lordly will.

It is great wisdom also to know how to refuse to yield to our feelings when they are unreasonable, how to check them and train them so that they may not become a danger to us. Some young people start out in life with the unfortunate and false idea that one should gratify feelings to the limit, and that there is something unhuman or unnatural about controlling them. The contrary is true. The feelings belong to the animal part of man, and although they are not wrong in themselves, they make beasts of men if they are unreasonably indulged. It is only by the inevitable self-discipline of controlling our feelings that we can become the persons we are meant to be, masters of ourselves and of our fate. One who is the slave of his feelings is no longer his own person.

Look back over your life up to this time, and see what part feelings have played in it, whether a worthy or an evil one. Ask yourself in how far you are now master of your feelings, how far they serve your purposes and help you to live a worthy and well-disciplined life. You will, no doubt, find reason to reproach yourself with yielding unduly to certain feelings, letting them tyrannize you and cause you to be unjust to others and to yourself.

Take definite resolves, and exert constant efforts to bring your feelings to be your servants and not your masters. This will make indescribably for your intelligence, your welfare, and your happiness.

Chapter Thirty-One

Have confidence in yourself

Overconfidence is a vice. Overtimidity is likewise a vice in the other direction. Between these two extremes lies the fine, wholesome, cheerful self-confidence that everyone should possess. Such confidence is not vanity and bragging, but it gives vigor to the mind, courage to the heart, and cheerfulness to the soul. Few things are more necessary for true and lasting success in life than this. One who is overconfident is rash, pretentious, and vain. He will not make the necessary efforts to succeed, but will rely on his own powers when he should depend on industry and hard work. He is likely to become soured from sad experience. He will not succeed where he expected to succeed, because he expects too much.

On the other hand, he who lacks sufficient confidence, who is overly timid and ever fearful, is still less likely to prosper. He is cowardly about trying new enterprises. He is diffident about undertaking responsibility. It is usually true that when a person thinks he cannot do a thing, he cannot.

The attitude with which one tackles a job has a great deal to do with his success or failure in it. The timid man is beaten before he begins to fight. He has failed before he starts his work. The overconfident man refuses to take the necessary precautions, to make the needful calculations, and to spend the right energy, and so he also fails. The man with firm, reasonable confidence goes at his task with energy and industry. He takes all the needful care, he makes all the necessary calculations, but he makes them with hopeful enthusiasm.

Some persons are by nature endowed with the spirit of confidence. They look on the bright side of everything. They have a substantial esteem of their own powers. This does not mean that they are vain or presumptuous, because they actually possess the qualities and capacities that make for confidence. These are the gifts of God, and it is right to recognize them, at the same time rendering thanks to the Giver.

Those who are blessed with the spirit of confidence should take good care to bring this disposition under the control of reason and not to allow it to degenerate into presumption, false confidence, or excessive self-reliance.

They are quite justified in admitting all the good qualities they possess and making the most of them, for this is what God intends. But they are very wrong to attribute these good qualities to themselves or to rely too much on their personal capacities and, therefore, to dispense themselves from hard work. Even the most talented persons have to toil and make efforts to use their talents. One who has very mediocre gifts, but a capacity for hard work will do more, be more, and achieve more in life than one who has very brilliant talents, but refuses to work to develop them.

One who is naturally timid, diffident, and lacks due confidence in himself ought to try to develop this necessary quality. He ought to look deliberately on the bright side of his character, to seek out and cultivate the gifts that he has by nature. A great deal depends, for such persons, on the choice of occupations in which they are qualified to succeed. If such a person takes up a task that is too hard for him or goes into work for which he is temperamentally and constitutionally unfit, the inevitable failure will increase his diffidence. If, however, he takes up something he can do well and works virtuously to achieve success, the very success itself will increase his self-confidence.

Well-ordered self-confidence is rooted in the will. One's feelings are very unsatisfactory and unreliable guides. They change like the wind. Now they incline us to be courageous; now they move us to timidity. A sensible person will never yield to his feelings when they tend to discourage him. He will bring everything to the bar of reason, and, if he finds that he has no reason to be discouraged, he will disregard his feelings.

Sometimes the criticism and opposition of others tend to discourage us and make us lose confidence. But it is virtuous to draw a profit from such opposition and not be hindered by it. If those who oppose us have good reasons for doing so, let us find out the reasons and correct them. If they are merely resisting us out of spite or enmity, let us arouse within us "the stern joy that warriors feel in foemen worthy of their steel."[10] Or, if these foemen be not worthy, let us at least use them as means to exercise ourselves in courageous resistance.

The skill that comes from practice in any art or occupation is a great source of confidence. Young people often lack self-confidence, because they are inexperienced. They have never tested themselves in the rough skirmishes of life, or never tried

[10] Sir Walter Scott, "The Lady of the Lake," canto 5, st. 10.

out their powers against opposition. But when they have had some practice in affairs, have won some victories, and have gained some skill, then confidence comes. Hence, by merely living on courageously, and exercising oneself in achievement, one gains more self-confidence.

Chapter Thirty-Two

Build a noble character

What more interesting and excellent purpose can a man set before him than to build up for himself a fine and noble personality? It is an excellent and admirable human achievement. One's personality, one's character, is himself; and the thought stirs the soul that you can remake yourself, perfect yourself, correct the evil within you, and fill out and develop the good within you, until you are a different person — finer, nobler, more excellently in accord with the ideals of human nature.

The building of character is a lifelong task. It requires the exercise of unremitting effort and weariless patience. It means rising up after falls, trying again after failures, never letting discouragement take hold of you. It means honest thought, careful observation of yourself and others, self-discipline, and courage. Yet all these things are possible while you are living your ordinary life, and they will bring with them the reward of the effort you make.

Sculptors who work in marble have a stubborn substance to conquer. Yet, what an inward delight they feel when, after all the careful planning, the stern effort of creation, and the patient struggle for self-expression, they see before them an exquisite work of art, beautiful and immortal, destined to receive the praise of men for generation after generation. Think of how Michelangelo felt when he rested his weary arms and gazed at the *Pietà*, one of the loveliest creations of human art. It had cost him immense pains, severe study, physical labor, and mental effort, but he had achieved it, and it was his.

Your efforts in character building are made with even more stubborn material perhaps, but far nobler: your will, your feelings, your intelligence, your habits, and your impulses, which must all be shaped, controlled, disciplined, and brought into harmony with an effort more careful and painstaking than is required to shape the gleaming marble with the sculptor's chisel.

Day after day, hour after hour, whether you wish it or not, you are at work on your character. Not a single deliberate action of your whole life is without its effect upon that character. You are so made that whatever action you perform tends to create or increase a habit. Yield to an evil impulse, and the evil habit grows stronger by just so much. Control that evil impulse, and in that very moment, you add just so much to the strength of your self-control. Perform an act of kindness to anyone, and at the moment, you become just so much kinder. Yield to an act of injustice, and your will tends to lean just so much more toward injustice.

You are different today from when you began to live, and much of that difference may be expressed in terms of the habits you have formed.

Moreover, the features of your character are changing from hour to hour. You are not even the person you were this morning. You are a little better or a little worse, in proportion as you have acted rightly or wrongly today. If your deeds today have been noble, it will be a little easier for you to be noble tomorrow. If your deeds today have been unworthy and base, you will have to struggle harder tomorrow to avoid baseness, and you will be a little readier to yield to temptation.

Many people nowadays have an ambition to build up a strong, symmetrical, athletic body, and there is only one way of doing this, and that is by systematic exercise. The same thing is true of your spirit, your mind, your intelligence, your memory, and your character. The only means to build up a noble and upright character is exercise — that is to say, the performance, day after day, of worthy actions, from good motives. The only way to correct the bad habits within you is precisely by means of exercise. As a person can strengthen his posture, round out his muscles, and add vigor to his whole constitution through skillfully chosen movements, so can you strengthen and harmonize your character by deliberately, day after day, going against your evil inclinations.

This discipline of the spirit is much nobler than the discipline of the body, because the finest, most athletic, healthful body will in a few years sink into dust. Nothing can preserve it in health and vigor for very long. But the spirit is immortal, and the building up of a fine character is not for time only but for eternity. The work you do on your character reaches forward beyond this life to all the ages to come.

If, then, you begin to train your character, to make it a leading pursuit of your life to study yourself and deliberately to cut down on what is excessive in you, to develop what is lacking, and to follow your good impulses and curb and restrain the evil ones, you will be benefiting not yourself alone, but everyone who comes in contact with you. Indeed, the result of this systematic and faithful training of your character will go far beyond your present influence and will bring help and strength to generations yet to come.

Biographical Note

Edward F. Garesché, S.J.

(1876-1960)

Born in St. Louis, Missouri, Edward Francis Garesché attended St. Louis University and Washington University and practiced law for two years before entering the Jesuit novitiate in Florrisant, Missouri. He was ordained a priest in 1912.

Fr. Garesché's priesthood was devoted to medical mission work and saw a vast literary output. He wrote seven volumes of poetry, for which he is best known, as well as twenty-four books, ten booklets, and numerous articles on subjects as diverse as prayer, meditation, inspiration, art, history, science, the teachings of the saints, sodality, education, pastoral theology, and nursing.

He founded *The Queen's Work,* a magazine of the Sodality of the Blessed Virgin, and edited *Hospital Progress* and *Medical Mission News,* a publication of the Catholic Medical Mission Board, of which he was president and director. Fr. Garesché also established the Knights of the Blessed Sacrament in the United States, began a Catholic Young Men's Association, and served as the spiritual director of the International Committee of the Catholic Federation of Nurses and of the Daughters of Mary, Health of the Sick.

How to Live Nobly and Well

Drawing on his wide-ranging interests and experience and with clear, inspiring words, Fr. Garesché offers his readers practical wisdom on how to find true success in life — that is, the attainment of holiness and happiness through good citizenship, prudent choices, and dutiful service to God and to others.

Sophia Institute Press®

Sophia Institute is a nonprofit institution that seeks to restore man's knowledge of eternal truth, including man's knowledge of his own nature, his relation to other persons, and his relation to God.

Sophia Institute Press® serves this end in numerous ways. It publishes translations of foreign works to make them accessible for the first time to English-speaking readers. It brings back into print books that have long been out of print. And it publishes important new books that fulfill the ideals of Sophia Institute. These books afford readers a rich source of the enduring wisdom of mankind.

Sophia Institute Press® makes these high-quality books available to the general public by using advanced technology and by soliciting donations to subsidize its general publishing costs.

Your generosity can help Sophia Institute Press® to provide the public with editions of works containing the enduring wisdom of the ages. Please send your tax-deductible contribution to the address on the following page.

The members of the Editorial Board of Sophia Institute Press® welcome questions, comments, and suggestions from all our readers.

For your free catalog, call:

Toll-free: 1-800-888-9344

or write:

Sophia Institute Press®

Box 5284, Manchester, NH 03108

or visit our website:

www.sophiainstitute.com

Sophia Institute is a tax-exempt institution
as defined by the Internal Revenue Code,
Section 501(c)(3). Tax I.D. 22-2548708.